Be a Neighbourhood Naturalist

Explore Nature with Activities and Experiments!

Labonie Roy Vena Kapoor Suhel Quader

JUGGERNAUT BOOKS
C-I-128, First Floor, Sangam Vihar, Near Holi Chowk,
New Delhi 110080, India

First published by Juggernaut Books 2025

Copyright © Nature Conservation Foundation 2025

10 9 8 7 6 5 4 3 2 1

ISBN: 9789353457396

All rights reserved. No part of this publication may be reproduced, transmitted, or stored in a retrieval system in any form or by any means without the written permission of the publisher.

The authors thank Bijal Vaccharajani, Jignasa Patel, Swati Sidhu, Abhisheka Krishnagopal, P. Jeganathan, Baheerathan Murugavel, Shama Quader, Kaveri Quader and *Brainwave Magazine*. Nandini Rajamani and Vinatha Viswanathan contributed to earlier versions of the text, with inputs from Abitha Anand, Anushree Bhattacharjee and Pavithra Sankaran. Additional thanks to Pixabay, Wikimedia Commons and Arindham Bhattacharya for images used and referenced in this book.

The authors are grateful to Wipro Foundation for support in preparing and printing this book.

Printed at Replika Press Pvt Ltd

Written by Labonie Roy, Vena Kapoor and Suhel Quader
Editing and scientific verification by Vena Kapoor and Suhel Quader
Art direction by Labonie Roy
Design and layout by Pratyush Gupta
Illustrations by Tanrus Studio and Upasana Chadha
Hand lettering by Tanrus Studio

Contents

Introduction	04
How to use this book	06
Why do geckos live in our homes?	08
What exactly is an insect?	10
How do ants work together?	12
Do all spider webs look the same?	14
What do plants eat?	16
Why do leaves look different from each other?	18
What are mushrooms?	20
Is there life underground?	22
What do baby insects look like?	24
Why do flies sit on our food?	26
Why do frogs like water?	28
How do some plants grow without soil?	30

How do animals breathe underwater?	**32**
Do smells have meanings?	**34**
How do plants protect themselves?	**36**
Why do flowers look so different from each other?	**38**
How do insects see the world?	**40**
Where are the flowers of fig trees?	**42**
Why do lice like living on our heads?	**44**
Do all plants come from seeds?	**46**
Which bird is singing?	**48**
What does sound tell us about our surroundings?	**50**
Why are some animals so colourful?	**52**
Why do moths prefer darkness to daylight?	**54**

Is that the animal I think it is?	**56**
Do all bees live in hives?	**58**
What's inside a wasp nest?	**60**
Do grasses only grow in parks and lawns?	**62**
Do all birds use twigs to build nests?	**64**
Why does a bird have different types of feathers?	**66**
What makes dragonflies such amazing pilots?	**68**
Why are there so many pigeons everywhere?!	**70**
Who pooped?	**72**
How do seeds reach new places?	**74**
What do bats really eat?	**76**
Which trees are growing around me?	**78**
Create a Nature Map	**80**
The team	**88**

Do you ever wonder why birds sing to each other, or why ants march in perfect lines? Or why some plants have green leaves and not others? We do, too!

As kids, we (Labonie, Suhel and Vena) went to school, read books and watched TV. We spent time playing with our friends, in our homes and outside. While doing this, we saw little things that you probably see as well: the occasional trail of ants on the floor, a big bird poop on a ledge or a tiny spider climbing up a wall. Everyday, normal things, right? But each of us **felt a spark** – a question that we just had to know the answer to! What were the ants looking for? What was in the bird's poop? Would the spider build a big or small web?

Sometimes, we could find an adult or a book that gave us the answers, but it was much more satisfying to **find out for ourselves**. One of us (Labonie) secretly left out piles of sugar in her house to see how ants find food. Another (Suhel) found seeds in bird poop and planted them to see what the bird had eaten. And another (Vena) carried a measuring tape everywhere to compare the sizes and shapes of different spider webs.

The more we noticed, the more questions we had, which led us on exciting explorations of nature around us. We observed, we created, we experimented; we played around with our ideas and worked with our hands. And we fell hopelessly in love with the amazing living beings that share our world. While doing so, we slowly **became naturalists**: people who are fascinated by the natural world and study it in one way or another. Eventually, we were lucky to be able to make nature our life's work – as artists, as scientists, as educators.

This book is for the naturalist in you! Through **questions about nature**, it guides you on an exploration of your surroundings, and the other living things that share them with you. Engaging experiments, observations, and creative activities will lead you to answers, and hopefully, to questions of your own. Through this book, you will:

Discover local nature: Through experiments, research projects, and stories, you'll discover your own natural habitat – your home and neighbourhood.

Spot, identify and learn: Identify common plants, animals and other living things, learn factual information about them, and expand your nature vocabulary.

Think like a scientist: Find out the whys and hows of nature by asking questions and finding out the answers.

Work with your head, heart and hands: Create science experiments using everyday materials found in your home.

Create a nature map: Build a record of the nature you have observed in your surroundings.

So dive in and begin your journey to
Be a Neighbourhood Naturalist!

How to use this book

This book guides you on an exploration of nature around you by asking questions and helping you find answers through observation and science experiments! You can use this book by yourself, or with a group, to explore nature together. It can also be used by teachers and educators, in classrooms or outdoor settings. Each topic is introduced over two pages: an Activity Sheet and a Fun Facts page. The Activity Sheet falls on the left-hand side, except in some cases where it's important to learn more about the topic before diving into the activity.

Activity Sheet

Find clues to answer the Nature Question by carrying out the activity and writing down your observations.

For groups: In groups or classroom settings where multiple copies of the book aren't available, you can provide a photocopy of the Activity Sheet for each person. The teacher or facilitator can use the book to conduct a lesson, and read out information from the Fun Facts page.

Nature Question: This is the question you will be finding the answers to through an experiment, craft or observation-based activity and some Fun Facts.

Nature Activity: Carry out this activity to see how nature works and find clues to answer the Nature Question.

You will need: All you need to do these activities are basic art materials and reusable waste from in and around your home or school. **(For groups:** Bring reusable materials needed for the activities from home).

What did you learn? Write down your observations and conclusions.

Take care: Be a responsible naturalist! This bubble tells you the safest ways to interact with nature during observations and activities.

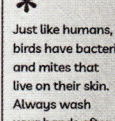

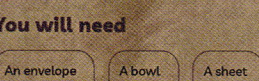

Things to keep in mind

1. When you venture out for observations, always keep this book and a pencil with you to write down what you see (and hear and smell!).

2. No measuring tape on hand? No problem! Use a unit you will remember – handspans, footsteps or even the length of your fingernail. You can use a string or a piece of paper to measure a distance (like the circumference of a tree) and compare it against a ruler or measuring tape later.

Fun Facts page
This page has some exciting scientific information about the topic. Using your observations and this information, can you answer the Nature Question?

Nature words: Learn a new word with each new topic.

For groups: Ask the Nature Question again after completing both pages – we are sure the answers will be very interesting!

Have you ever seen a lizard on your ceiling and wondered:

Why do geckos live in our homes?

Did you know you share your home with a wild predator? This fascinating creature is none other than the Common House Gecko. They can be seen scurrying across walls and ceilings, and may make surprise appearances while you reach for your favourite book from the shelf or pick up the towel hanging in your bathroom. These remarkable reptiles are comfortable living almost anywhere inside our homes – but why do they like it so much?

>
> House geckos are harmless and do not bite! When they feel threatened, geckos can drop their tails to distract a predator. Their tails wiggle even after getting detached, and the geckos make a quick getaway. For their safety, do not try to catch or handle them.

You will need
- A watch or timer
- A sheet of paper and 2 coloured markers/pencils

1. Imagine looking down on your house from directly above, as if you were a bird. You also have a special superpower – X-ray vision so that you can look through your ceiling. How does your house look? Draw a map of all the rooms and label each room.

2. Try and find geckos living in your home. You may find them on walls present near lightbulbs, on screen doors, and behind picture frames or other hiding places. A sure sign of a gecko is their poop which looks like a black grain of rice with a white dot at one end.

3. For observations between 9.00 a.m. and 6.00 p.m., choose one coloured marker to write with, and for 6.00 p.m. to your bedtime, choose the other colour.

4. Every time you see a gecko, look at the time and mark where you saw the gecko on your map with an 'X' using the right pen. Write down the date, time and what the gecko was doing.

5. Observe and note what you see for 5 days.

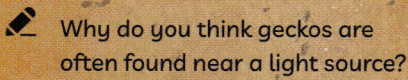

Gecko poop

✏️ Why do you think geckos are often found near a light source?
....
....
....
....
....
....
....

✏️ At what time were the geckos most active?
....
....
....
....
....

It's all about food!

While observing house geckos, you may have noticed that they were hunting for food. Geckos are expert hunters and spend most of their time awake catching ants, mosquitos, spiders, beetles, moths and other small creatures they find. They flick their sticky, flexible tongues, faster than the eye can see, to catch their prey. Geckos don't have eyelids, so their tongues also come in handy to clean their eyes!

What's common among all the creatures geckos like to eat? You may have noticed them in or around your house, or in other indoor spaces. At night, lights attract insects, which is a feast for the gecko! Indoors, geckos are also protected from animals that want to eat them, like birds, cats and snakes.

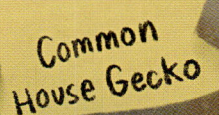
Common House Gecko

Adapting to urban life

Many species of geckos have adapted to urban environments.

You may find darker-coloured geckos on darker surfaces like tree trunks and lamp posts.

Lighter-coloured geckos can be spotted on walls.

They are also famous for being able to walk upside down on most surfaces without falling, thanks to thousands of tiny hairs on their feet that act like velcro.

A scientist who studies amphibians or reptiles like geckos is called a **herpetologist**.

Have you ever looked at a little bug and wondered:

What exactly is an insect?

There is an astonishing variety of 'bugs' and 'creepy-crawlies' around us. Millipedes get around on many little legs, but ants have only six. Beetles have smooth, shiny bodies, but worms are soft and squishy. Butterflies flutter by on papery wings, but slugs and snails slowly make their way on a trail of slime. Are all these different animals a part of the grand group we call insects? What exactly is an 'insect'?

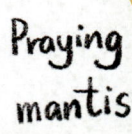

Praying mantis

✎ Write down the words that come to mind when you think of 'insects'.

Look carefully at these pictures and note your observations.

Common Mormon Butterfly

Indian Black Ant

If possible, try and find a real (live or dead) insect and compare it with the insects in the photos above.

✎ How many legs does each have?
Butterfly ....
Ant ....

✎ How does each move around?
Butterfly ....
Ant ....

✎ Do they have distinctly separate sections of their bodies? How many such sections do you see?
Butterfly ....
Ant ....

✎ Observe the heads closely. Do you see any similarities?
....
....
....

✎ Using your observations, make a list of features common to both of them:
....
....
....
....
....
....

Butterflies and ants clearly have a lot in common – with each other and also with a whole group of animals called insects.

Six legs (three pairs): Each leg also has clearly identifiable sections.

Body divided into distinct sections: The bodies of insects are divided into three parts, called the head, thorax and abdomen. These look slightly different in different insects. The head has the eyes, mouth and antennae. The thorax is where the insect's legs and wings are attached. The abdomen is softer and sometimes covered by the wings. This is where insects digest their food, and – you guessed it – make poop!

Paired antennae: All insects have a pair of antennae (we might know them as 'feelers') on their heads, which they use to smell and find food.

Compound eyes: All insects have a pair of compound eyes, each of which is made up of hundreds or thousands of tiny units.

Hard outer skeleton: Insects have a hard outer skeleton to protect their bodies. This layer makes some insects, like ants, wasps, and beetles, look smooth and shiny.

Paired wings: Most adult insects have one or two pairs of wings. Some are thin and transparent, while others have beautiful colours and patterns.

*What does a compound eye look like? Find out on **page 42**.*

Banana Stem Weevil

Which of these are insects?

- ☐ Six legs
- ☐ Three sections
- ☐ Paired antennae
- ☐ Compound eyes
- ☐ Hard outer skin
- ☐ Paired wings

Red Dwarf Honey Bee

- ☐ Six legs
- ☐ Three sections
- ☐ Paired antennae
- ☐ Compound eyes
- ☐ Hard outer skin
- ☐ Paired wings

Spotted Locust

✏️ An animal that has ..... legs, ... body segments and paired wings is called an **insect**.

- ☐ Six legs
- ☐ Three sections
- ☐ Paired antennae
- ☐ Compound eyes
- ☐ Hard outer skin
- ☐ Paired wings

Chrysilla volupe jumping spider

Indrella ampulla land snail

- ☐ Six legs
- ☐ Three sections
- ☐ Paired antennae
- ☐ Compound eyes
- ☐ Hard outer skin
- ☐ Paired wings

You may have observed that spiders and millipedes have some similarities to insects – making them cousins but not true insects. Snails and worms are entirely different, and much further away in the family tree. So, the next time you see a 'bug' or 'creepy-crawly', think through your list – is it an insect?

Have you ever seen a group of ants walking in a straight line and wondered:

How do ants work together?

Ants live in large groups called colonies with anywhere between thousands and millions of ants. They all work together towards the same goal – making sure they have a safe home and lots of food so that the colony can grow. Most ant species also build elaborate nests to house the colony – tall anthills, underground tunnels or even hanging nests made from leaves! If you have ever done a group project or played sports as part of a team, you know that it takes a lot of conversations and coordination to work together to get things done. So how do ants do it?

Yes, some ants do bite, but only to protect themselves! So, for your own safety as well as the ants', do not touch them and watch where you step!

Ghost Ant

You will need
- A spoonful of food (sugar, atta, rice or a chopped boiled egg)
- A watch or timer

1. Look around for a trail of ants in your home, or open spaces nearby. Your kitchen, near a food source or the base of a tree are good places to start.

2. Place a spoonful of food 2 handspans away from the ant trail you have found. Note the time on your watch.

3. How long does it take for ants to find the food? If they don't find the food in 5 minutes, move it a little closer and note the time on your watch again. How does the first ant behave after finding the food? What do the other ants do when they find it?

4. Check again every 2 minutes, note how many ants are at the food as well as the details of their behaviour. Are there more or fewer ants than the last time you checked? How are they carrying the food? Note how many ants are there. Observe for 10 minutes, or if you can, until the food is gone.

✏️ How do you think the first few ants discovered the food?

....
....
....
....

✏️ How do you think the other ants found out about it?

....
....
....
....

✏️ **Number of ants**

after 2 minutes ....
after 4 minutes ....
after 6 minutes ....
after 8 minutes ....
after 10 minutes ....

Ant language

Similar to how you speak with your friends, ants have their own ways of communicating. While observing ants, you may notice that they use their antennae to sweep the surface they are walking on or to tap each other when they meet. Ants can smell and feel through their antennae and even their feet, and communicate using scents. When a worker ant finds food, she rushes back to the nest, leaving a trail of scent by tapping her abdomen on the ground. Other ants use their antennae to tap her and catch the scent, then trace it back to the food. Some types of ants even make high-pitched sounds by scraping their legs against their bodies. Using these methods of communication, ants work so well together that scientists consider ant colonies a **super-organism**, because the whole colony functions as one.

Do other animals also use scents to communicate? Find out on page 36.

Common Black Ant

Inside an ant nest

When observing an ant colony, you may have noticed that some ants from the same colony look different from each other. Some have bigger heads and mouthparts, and in the rainy season, you may even see winged ants! Most ant colonies have four types of ants, each with a specific responsibility.

Drones are winged male ants. When the time comes, the drone and princess ants fly out of the nest to mate. The drone dies soon after, while the princess sheds her wings and lays her eggs in a safe place to start a new colony, becoming its queen.

Each colony has one or more **queen ants**. The queen lives in a special chamber in the nest and is the only ant who can lay eggs – all the other ants in a colony are her children.

Worker ants make up the majority of a colony – they go out to find and bring back food, and care for the eggs and young ones. All worker ants are female.

Soldier ants guard the nest and protect the colony from harm with their powerful jaws. All soldier ants are female.

A scientist who studies ants is called a **myrmecologist**.

Have you ever seen a delicate circular spider web and wondered:

Do all spider webs look the same?

At first glance (before you get entangled), all spider webs may look similar. But their webs vary from simple flat sheets to silken cities! Not all spiders build webs, but they all have the ability to produce seemingly endless quantities of fine silk. Each spider can make several kinds of silk that it uses for different purposes – to wrap its prey, as a protective cover for its eggs, as an anchor, and even to lay scented trails for its mates to follow. And of course, spiders use their stickiest silk to trap insects and other prey in complex webs.

Most spiders are harmless to humans and would prefer to be left alone to catch insects in peace. It's best to avoid touching spiders or their webs!

When an insect flies into a spider web, it sticks to the silk, entangling itself as it tries to get free. The movements make the strands of the web vibrate, alerting the spider to exactly where the insect is. The spider scuttles smoothly across, its hairy legs protecting it from sticking to the silk. It bites the prey, injecting it with immobilising venom. Using a thicker silk, the spider wraps up its food – to be eaten immediately or later!

Spiders may be small, but they can travel large distances. Spiders shoot strands of silk into the air, which are caught by the wind that then whisks them off to new places. This is called **ballooning**.

Signature spider web

You will need

- Sheets of paper
- A pencil

1. Take a walk in a nearby park, garden or an undisturbed patch of plants. Look carefully for signs of silken webs. You may find them on plants, grass or even on the ground.

2. Observe each web you find. Based on what you know, what type of web is it? Tick the type of web you have seen. Draw and label each web – and don't forget to look for the spider!

☐ **Orb webs:** Most commonly found outdoors, and in movies and storybooks. These are neatly circular and have lines coming outward from the centre, like a bicycle wheel. The web is woven in a single spiral, and the silk lines are close together to catch flying insects such as bees and flies. Giant wood spiders can build orb webs up to a metre wide, strong enough to accidentally trap small birds that fly by! Signature spiders are a family of orb weavers that use a thick type of silk and weave an X at the centre of their webs.

☐ **Cobwebs:** Commonly found indoors – in the corners of ceilings or under furniture. These tangled webs are built by the commonly found long-legged house spiders to catch small insects such as flies and ants.

☐ **Tent webs:** Shaped like a dome or tent with a silken floor, commonly found among plants. The spider typically hunts from the top of the web. Some tent web spiders lay their eggs in a strand, much like a necklace, at the centre of the web.

☐ **Funnel and sheet webs:** Sheets of closely woven silk that form a funnel-shaped structure towards the back. The spider hides inside the funnel, waiting for an unsuspecting insect to walk across the extended silken sheet. When it feels the silk threads vibrating, it darts out, catches its prey and drags it back into the funnel.

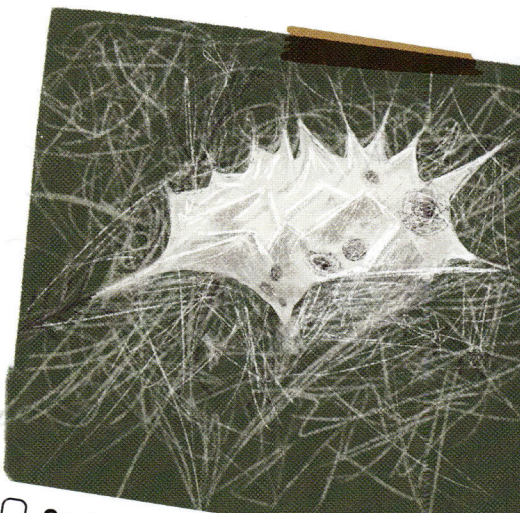

☐ **Social webs:** Some spiders work together to build giant webs. These can host thousands of individuals who also share the prey caught in the web. Their webs can cover entire shrubs and sometimes, even trees!

While gazing up a towering tree, have you ever wondered:

What do plants eat?

From a tiny seed to a giant tree, plants continue growing throughout their lives. But how do they get all the nutrition required to grow so big without hands, mouths and being unable to move around?

You will need

- 3 spoonfuls of coriander (or mustard) seeds
- 3 identical containers filled with soil and compost (or moist soil from a garden or park)
- 2 cardboard boxes big enough to cover the containers
- A pair of scissors
- A marker pen or sticker

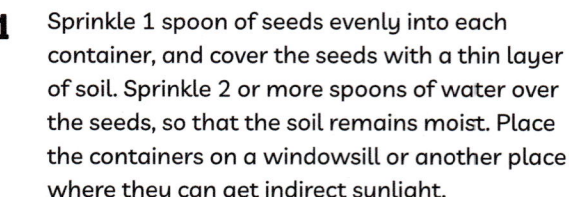

1. Sprinkle 1 spoon of seeds evenly into each container, and cover the seeds with a thin layer of soil. Sprinkle 2 or more spoons of water over the seeds, so that the soil remains moist. Place the containers on a windowsill or another place where they can get indirect sunlight.

2. All your seeds now have soil, compost, water and air. Mark the first container as 'Sunlit Seeds'.

3. Using the scissors, carefully punch 10–15 holes on one side of a cardboard box. Widen each hole using a pen so that your finger can fit through. Cover the second container with this box and mark it as 'Partly Sunlit Seeds'.

4. Cover the third container with the remaining box, making sure no light reaches the seeds. Mark the box as 'Sunless Seeds'.

5. Make sure to gently water all three containers everyday, but put the boxes back on the Partly Sunlit Seeds and Sunless Seeds immediately after watering them!

6. Continue to water and observe them until the Sunlit Seeds have grown into tiny plants a couple of inches tall with 2 leaves. Now, remove the boxes from over the other 2 containers and compare the growth.

7. After the experiment, you can harvest the plants by cutting the stems just above the soil. Use them in salads or other dishes!

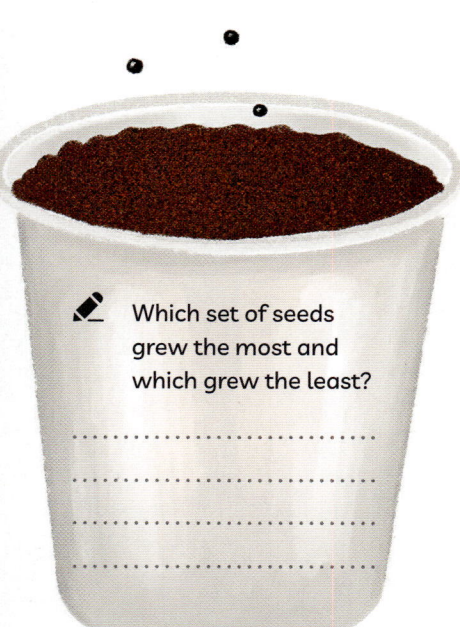

Which set of seeds grew the most and which grew the least?
....
....

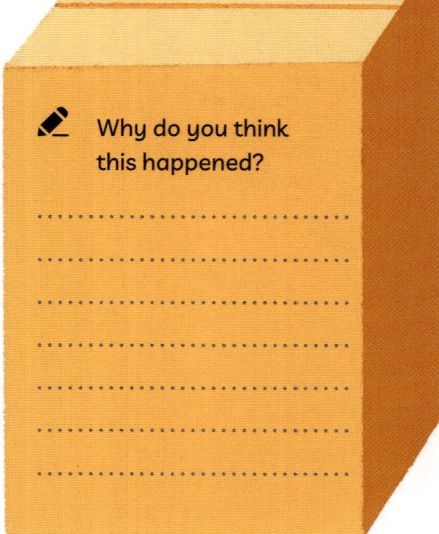

Why do you think this happened?
....
....
....
....
....
....

What happened to the Partly Sunlit Seeds?
....
....
....
....
....
....

Air, water and sunlight!

Unlike humans and other animals, plants seem to need only fresh air, soil and water to grow. But through your experiment, you may have realised that there's something else they need – sunlight! While the Sunlit Seeds grew into leafy green seedlings, the Sunless Seeds grew very slowly, or maybe not at all. They may also have grown thin and white stalks without leaves. Between the two sets of seeds, the only difference was that one had sunlight and the other didn't! You may also have observed your Partly Sunlit Seeds leaning towards the side of the box with holes as they grew into baby plants. The tiny plants were growing towards the sunlight!

Why do plants need sunlight and how do they grow without eating? The answer: plants use sunlight to make their own food! The leaf is the plant's kitchen where all the magic happens. Using minerals from the soil, plants produce a green pigment called chlorophyll. Chlorophyll makes plants green and also has the important job of collecting sunlight. Using sunlight as energy, water from the soil and carbon dioxide from the air are cooked together to create plant food! During this process, plants release life-giving oxygen into the air.

> The process by which plants make their own food using water, carbon dioxide and sunlight is called **photosynthesis**.

From sunlight to you

All living beings need food to grow. As we have seen, plants use energy from sunlight to make their own food. Animals can't do this, so they eat plants for energy. Some animals, called herbivores, eat only plants. Others, called carnivores, eat animals who eat plants. Omnivores (like humans) eat plants and other animals.

The process of energy travelling from the sun to an animal's body is called the **food chain**. At your next meal, try to trace each ingredient back to sunlight. You might be surprised at how many steps it takes for the energy from sunlight to reach your plate!

A food chain

A Black-winged Kite eats the myna

A Myna eats the grasshopper

A grasshopper eats the grass.

Grass gains energy from sunlight through photosynthesis.

Have you ever looked at a variety of plants and wondered:

Why do leaves look different from each other?

Leaves are where the magic happens in a plant – they take in carbon dioxide from the air, water and nutrients from the soil, mix in a little bit of sunshine and make plant food! But if all leaves do the same thing, why do they look so different from each other?

> *****
>
> Some plants may have sticky, white sap that oozes out when a stem is injured and broken. Avoid contact with hands and eyes, and wash your hands.
>
> 🔍 *What could this sap be? Find out on **page 36**.*

You will need

A paper and pencil

1. Collect leaves from 5 plants around you. Try to make sure that they look as different from each other as possible in terms of colour, shape and size.

2. Create a simple observation sheet to compare the leaves, with the following information:

| Trace the outline of the leaf and draw the pattern of the veins. | Length of the leaf in centimetres (cm) – measure along the central rib from base to tip. | Colour description – For both upper and lower surfaces, what colour are they most similar to? | Is the surface shiny or dull? |

3. Try to find out what the plant is called – ask your friends, family members, and community workers like gardeners, domestic workers and security guards.

✏️ What do all these leaves have in common?

....
....
....
....

Colour me green

The leaves are often called the 'kitchen of the plant' – this is where all the ingredients mix to make plant food. Plants contain a green pigment called **chlorophyll** that absorbs sunlight and uses that energy to make food out of air and water. Even if the leaves you collect are mostly red, yellow, brown or purple, they contain some chlorophyll. As the leaves of a plant age or die, the chlorophyll degrades and the leaf turns yellow or brown.

Big and small

To soak up as much sunlight as possible, some plants have huge leaves. Banana trees or Colocasia plants have only a few leaves, but they are huge – often longer than your arm. Other plants like the Gulmohar tree have hundreds of leaves with thousands of tiny leaflets to help absorb sunlight.

Gulmohar

> A leaf made up of many tiny 'leaflets' joined to a single stem is called a **compound leaf**.

Keeping the moisture in (and out!)

Plants draw water through their roots right up to their leaves. While observing your leaves, you would have noticed a pattern of lines – these are the veins of the leaves. They are like plumbing pipes that transport water through the leaf. Some of this water is used by the leaves to make food for the plants and the rest is released into the air.

Some plants like the rubber tree have a shiny, waxy coating on their leaves to prevent drying. Shade-loving plants have softer, non-waxy leaves.

Plants like cacti and succulents grow in dry places and need to save as much water as they can. To protect the water stored in their stems, they have converted their leaves into spines.

Some plants have also adapted to handle heavy rainfall. Their leaves have developed narrow tips called drip tips, which let water roll off easily.

Plants shape their leaves so that they can make the maximum amount of food while staying healthy and comfortable in their surroundings – whether it's hot, cold, rainy or dry. In fact, if you move a plant from one space to another, it may shed all its leaves and grow new leaves to suit its surroundings better. Try moving an indoor plant outside to a space with soft sunlight and observe what happens over a few months!

While eating a delicious dish made of mushrooms, have you ever wondered:

What are mushrooms?

Are mushrooms plants or animals? It may surprise you to know that mushrooms belong to a big family of organisms called fungi! Fungi are everywhere – growing on tree trunks, black splotches on walls, ingredients in life-saving medicines and even on our plates. But what makes fungi different from plants and animals?

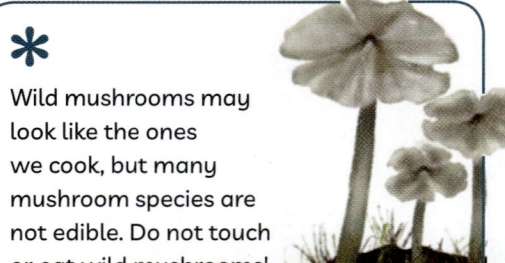

* Wild mushrooms may look like the ones we cook, but many mushroom species are not edible. Do not touch or eat wild mushrooms!

You will need

- A clean glass bottle with a lid
- A slice of bread or a chapati
- A small bowl of water

1. With your fingers, sprinkle about 2 teaspoons of water onto the bread or chapati.
2. Put the bread into the glass bottle. You can break the bread into smaller pieces.
3. Tighten the lid and put the glass bottle into a dark cupboard. This activity works best if the bottle is also in a warm place.
4. Note the changes on the bread everyday for a week or 10 days.

If you notice blue-green or fluffy white patches, congratulations! You have grown a fungus!

Be careful: Do not open the bottle at all during the experiment. After you have finished observing your fungus, cover your nose and mouth with a mask or scarf, and empty the bottle among the plants where ants can find and eat the bread. Wash the bottle carefully before uncovering your nose and mouth.

✏ Where do you think the fungus came from?

✏ Why did we ask you to cover your nose and mouth while opening the bottle?

💬 The scientific study of fungi is called **mycology**. Mycologists study fungi to understand them, and research how to make better food and more effective medicines from them.

A fun(gus) family

During the activity, did you observe a fungus growing on your bread or chapati? These types of fungi, called moulds, are the cousins of mushrooms and often grow on old or rotting food. Fungi absorb food from whatever they grow on. When they are fully grown, they form fruits – but not like the ones we see on plants. The mushrooms we eat are the fruits of a fungus. These fruits release millions of tiny spores – which are like the seeds of a fungus. Spores are small and light, and float around in the air. The spores of some fungi can be dangerous for our health because they are small enough to enter our lungs. When they land on a moist surface, they can grow into fungi.

Button mushrooms

Button mushrooms like this as well as many other mushrooms are commonly eaten around the world.

Yeast

A tiny fungus that is used in baking to make fluffy bread and cakes. Some types of yeasts are even found living between people's toes!

Worm-eating fungi

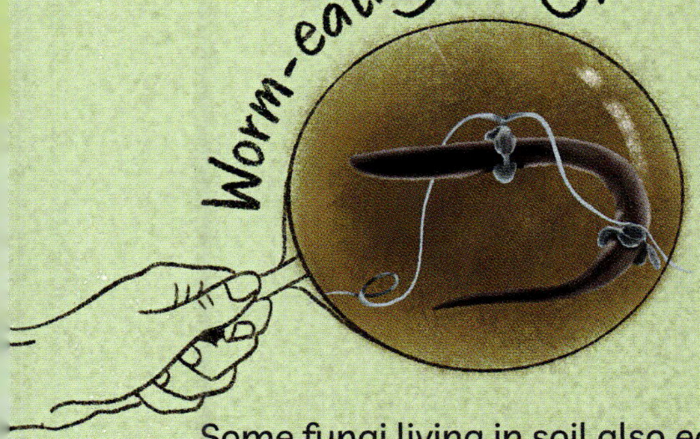

Some fungi living in soil also eat tiny worms! They capture them in circular traps that tighten as the worm tries to wriggle through, or through sticky glue that catches the worm. After catching the worm, the fungus slowly eats it.

Bracket fungi

Bracket fungi look like small shelves and can be seen growing on tree trunks. They break down tough wood for smaller insects and animals to eat and live in.

Glowing mushrooms

A few fungi even glow in the dark! They grow on the branches of trees in forests around the world and produce a green light in the dark. One variety of glowing mushroom in the forests of Meghalaya is so bright that people use the branches as natural torches at night.

Have you ever watched an earthworm wriggle into the soil and wondered:

Is there life underground?

Birds, bees, butterflies, plants, flowers – we see so much variety in nature around us. But there's also a whole hidden world in the soil under our feet!

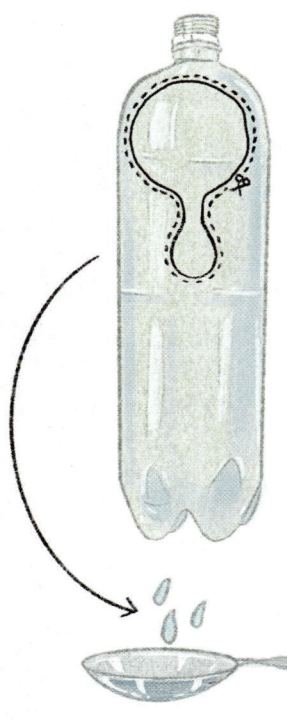

You will need

- A measuring tape or scale
- A small trowel or some other digging tool
- 2 sheets of newspaper
- A pair of scissors
- A marker pen
- A spoon
- 2 matching transparent containers, filled halfway with water
- A magnifying glass or a phone camera with zoom. (To make your own magnifying glass you will need an empty clear plastic bottle with a curved top).

1. During this activity, you will be observing soil under a magnifying glass. If you don't have a magnifying glass, use the following steps to make one of your own.
   a) Using a marker, make an 8 cm-wide circle on the curved part of the plastic bottle.
   b) Ask an adult to help you cut the circle out. It should look like a shallow bowl.
   c) Fill the bowl halfway with clear water and your homemade magnifying glass is ready!

2. Find a patch of moist soil, preferably under shrubs or with plants growing out of it. Mark a patch of soil that's at least 10 cm by 10 cm. Using your trowel, dig up the soil to 15 cm depth and place the soil on the newspaper.

3. Spread the soil out on the newspaper, remove stones and crumble any clumps of soil. Observe any bug activity with your magnifying glass.

4. Repeat this activity with a dry patch of soil without any small plants or grass. You may find it in a park playground or by a street.

5. Take 3 handfuls of the moist soil and using the spoon, mix them into one of the containers with water. Do the same with the dry soil. If there are any bugs in the water, pick them out quickly with the spoon so that they don't drown!

6. Let the containers sit undisturbed for 15 minutes. Using the spoon, examine what has settled at the bottom of each container and what is floating at the top.

✏️ Was there a difference in the insect activity between the 2 types of soil?
....
....
....
....
....

✏️ What was floating in the water, and what had settled at the bottom?
....
....
....

✏️ Which container had more floating stuff?
....

💬 When living things like plants and animals die, their bodies are naturally broken down into tiny bits that mix back into soil or water. This process is called **decomposition.**

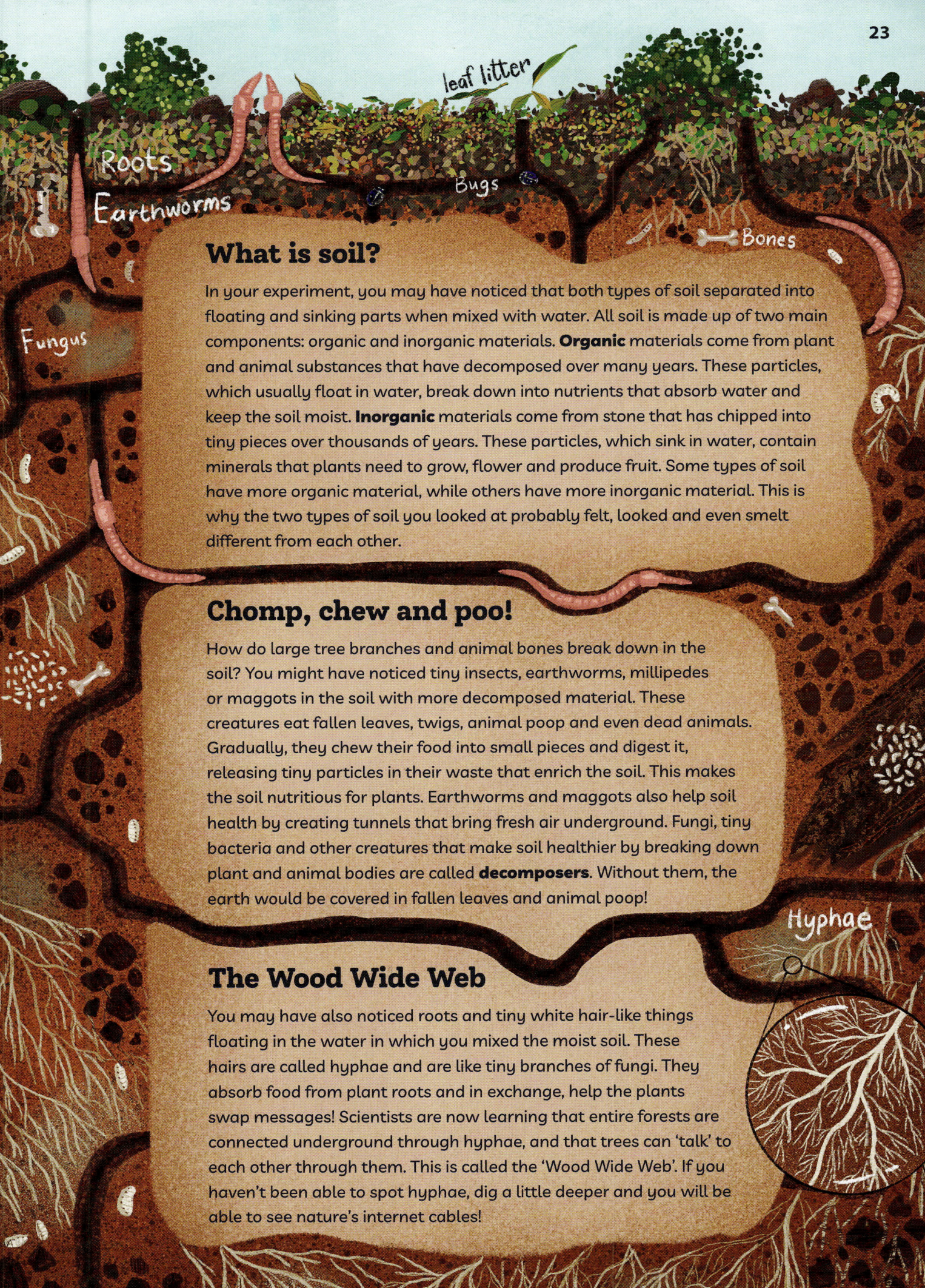

What is soil?

In your experiment, you may have noticed that both types of soil separated into floating and sinking parts when mixed with water. All soil is made up of two main components: organic and inorganic materials. **Organic** materials come from plant and animal substances that have decomposed over many years. These particles, which usually float in water, break down into nutrients that absorb water and keep the soil moist. **Inorganic** materials come from stone that has chipped into tiny pieces over thousands of years. These particles, which sink in water, contain minerals that plants need to grow, flower and produce fruit. Some types of soil have more organic material, while others have more inorganic material. This is why the two types of soil you looked at probably felt, looked and even smelt different from each other.

Chomp, chew and poo!

How do large tree branches and animal bones break down in the soil? You might have noticed tiny insects, earthworms, millipedes or maggots in the soil with more decomposed material. These creatures eat fallen leaves, twigs, animal poop and even dead animals. Gradually, they chew their food into small pieces and digest it, releasing tiny particles in their waste that enrich the soil. This makes the soil nutritious for plants. Earthworms and maggots also help soil health by creating tunnels that bring fresh air underground. Fungi, tiny bacteria and other creatures that make soil healthier by breaking down plant and animal bodies are called **decomposers**. Without them, the earth would be covered in fallen leaves and animal poop!

The Wood Wide Web

You may have also noticed roots and tiny white hair-like things floating in the water in which you mixed the moist soil. These hairs are called hyphae and are like tiny branches of fungi. They absorb food from plant roots and in exchange, help the plants swap messages! Scientists are now learning that entire forests are connected underground through hyphae, and that trees can 'talk' to each other through them. This is called the 'Wood Wide Web'. If you haven't been able to spot hyphae, dig a little deeper and you will be able to see nature's internet cables!

Have you ever looked at a tiny ladybug and wondered:

What do baby insects look like?

We see insects everywhere – in our homes, around our houses, underwater and even up in the air. But are we looking at baby insects or fully grown ones?

You will need

- 1 cup of fruit or vegetable peels, or other green scraps from your kitchen
- 4 pieces of sweet fruit
- 1 cup of soil or compost
- A plastic box with a lid
- A pair of scissors

1. Make 5–6 holes in the lid of the plastic box with the scissors. The holes should be big enough to push a pencil through.
2. Mix the green scraps and soil or compost in the plastic box.
3. Place the pieces of fruit on top and close the lid.
4. Leave the box outdoors in a well-ventilated place where it won't be disturbed.
5. Open the box and check inside every alternate day for a week. Note any changes and insect activity that you see.
6. After a week, you can bury the contents of the box so that they can decompose in the soil.

On each occasion that you opened the box, how did the box smell? Did you spot anything moving inside? What do you think it was?

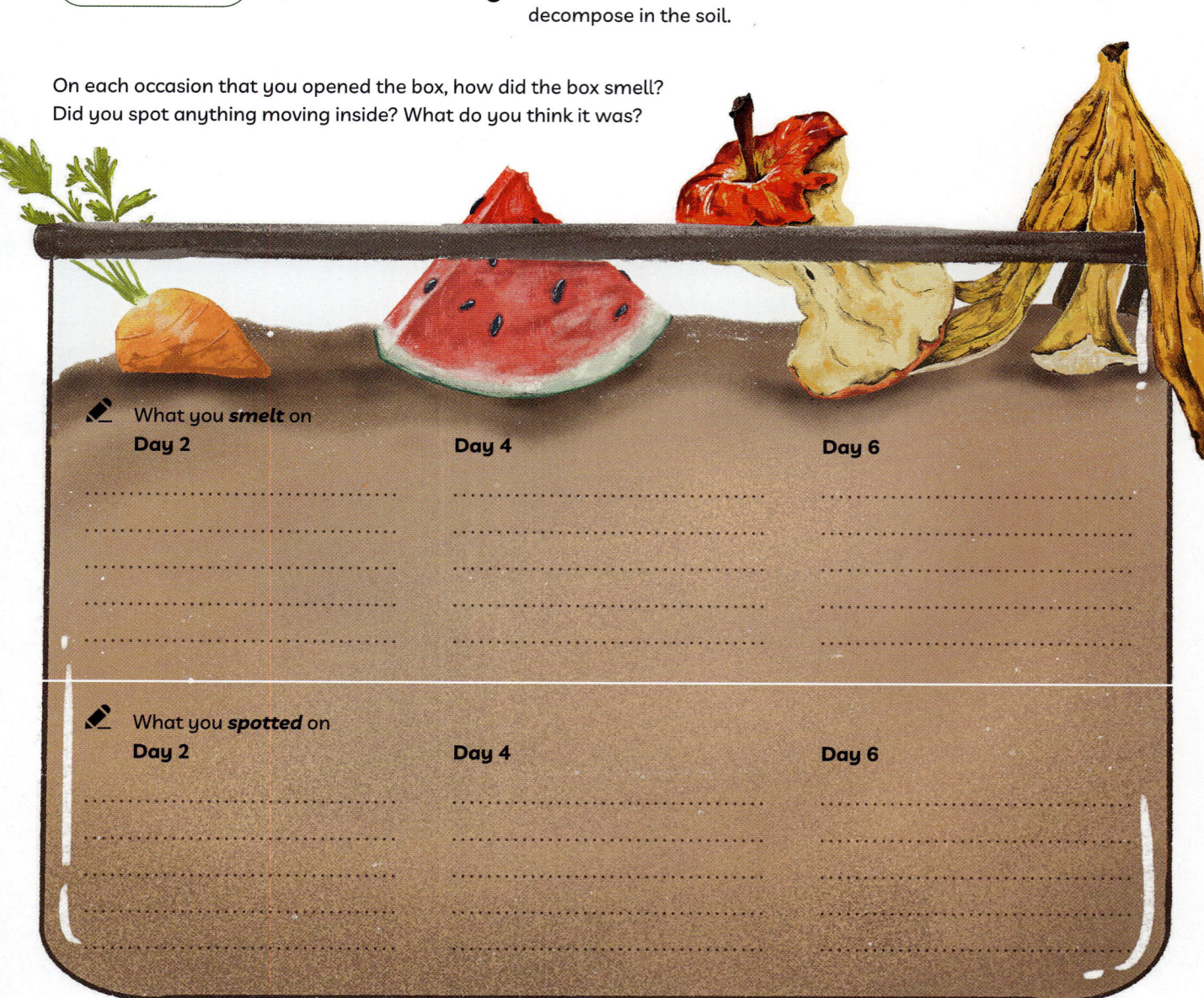

What you *smelt* on
Day 2 | Day 4 | Day 6

What you *spotted* on
Day 2 | Day 4 | Day 6

Black Soldier Fly

Adult soldier fly emerging from pupal case

The egg

In the later days of your experiment, you might not have been eager to check on the box because of the strong rotting smell. However, the stink is a welcome invitation for some insects, like flies! When they find food that tastes and smells good to them, they may use it as a place to lay eggs so that their young have a yummy meal to eat when they hatch. All insects lay eggs and spend a lot of time finding or creating a safe place for them.

The larva

Like all insects, flies hatch from eggs into something that looks very different from the adult. You may have noticed white, wriggling, worm-like creatures among the food scraps you left in the box. These are baby flies, also called maggots. The babies of many other insects, such as beetles, bees, wasps and ants, look quite similar. These baby insects are called larvae, and they come in many shapes and colours. Moth and butterfly caterpillars are also types of larvae and can be green, black or red; and smooth or hairy!

The pupa and the adult

Larvae need time and a lot of food to grow into adults. Some, like maggots and caterpillars, can move around and find their own food. Others, such as the larvae of colony-living insects like ants, bees and wasps, are fed by the adults. Once they are ready, larvae form a protective covering around their bodies. In this stage, they are called pupae. Inside this covering, their bodies completely transform, and they come out as adults!

Tawny Coster butterfly

Metamorphosis is the process of how an insect's body transforms after hatching, stage by stage, into its adult form. Most insects go through some form of metamorphosis to reach adulthood.

A butterfly pupa is called a chrysalis

Have you ever seen a fly buzzing around your plate and wondered:

Why do flies sit on our food?

You probably see a few flies every day – they love hanging around human homes so much that one kind is even called a 'Housefly'. They buzz around fruit bowls and food containers, and nearly always avoid being swatted. But why do flies sit on our food?

You will need

- A tall transparent glass or a glass jar
- A plain sheet of paper
- Sticky tape
- An overripe banana

1. Slice the banana and place 2 pieces at the bottom of the glass.

2. Roll the sheet of paper into a cone, with a coin-sized opening at the narrow end. Tape the paper so that the cone doesn't open.

3. Place the cone into the mouth of the glass. Adjust it so that the wide end fits the opening of the glass without any gaps.

4. Your fly jar is ready! Place it in your kitchen or outdoors, in a place where you have noticed flies. Note the time.

5. Observe every half an hour for the next 3 hours and note any insect activity along with the time. If you see flies in the jar, watch them very closely – what do they do around the banana slices?

6. Flies and other insects won't be able to get out of the jar on their own. When you have finished your observations, remove the paper cone so that they can fly out.

✎ Why did we ask you to use an overripe banana? How do you think the flies knew the banana was there?

....
....
....
....

✎ Were the flies eating the banana? Did you see any body parts that looked like a mouth or teeth?

....
....
....

A tasty treat under the feet

Flies are enthusiastic foodies and make a meal of almost anything – especially strong-smelling food and waste! Flies use their stubby but sensitive antennae to smell. Sweet-smelling fruits, like bananas, attract flies, especially tiny red-eyed fruit flies. You may have noticed the flies walking around on the piece of banana. Adult flies taste through their feet, making every walk a tasting course! They don't have a tongue or teeth. Instead, they use their tube-like mouth, called a proboscis, to suck up liquids. If they come across solid food that they like, they spit out digestive juices which soften and liquefy their meal, and slurp it up like a smoothie!

House fly

Experts of the air

Flies are actually a whole group of insects who are experts of the air – there's a hint in their name! There are many kinds of flies around us – drone flies, fruit flies, flower flies, crane flies and even mosquitos. Some, like mosquitoes and horse flies, may drink human blood and can be carriers of disease. Other flies sip nectar from flowers and pollinate wild plants and crops including mangoes and apples.

All flies have only a single pair of wings, whereas other insects have two pairs. Instead of a second pair of wings, flies have small, club-shaped organs called halteres. While flying, halteres help with balance, direction, sharp turns and even upside-down landings! Flies are covered in small hairs that help them sense changes in the direction of the wind, including when we move our hands to swat them. This is why flies often rub their front legs – they aren't planning something evil, just making sure their hairs are free of dirt so they can sense you coming!

Drone fly

Crane fly

Halteres

Flies, butterflies, moths and many other insects have a tube-like mouth to help them drink liquid food. This is called a **proboscis**.

Have you ever heard frogs croaking on a rainy night and wondered:

Why do frogs like water?

A rustle among the grass, a quiet croak from a bathroom corner, or a *sploosh* in a puddle – you may have seen or heard a frog without even realising it! They were once a common sight in our cities and towns, and still appear magically in rainy weather to enchant us with their croaky songs. But where do frogs go for the rest of the year? And why do they come out only when it rains?

Best of both worlds

Baby frogs look very different from adult frogs! They hatch from eggs into tadpoles. Tadpoles live underwater and breathe through gills, like fish do. As they grow, they develop lungs and legs, lose their tail and eventually leave the water to live on land. Adult frogs can still swim in water and are often found in and around streams, ponds and lakes.

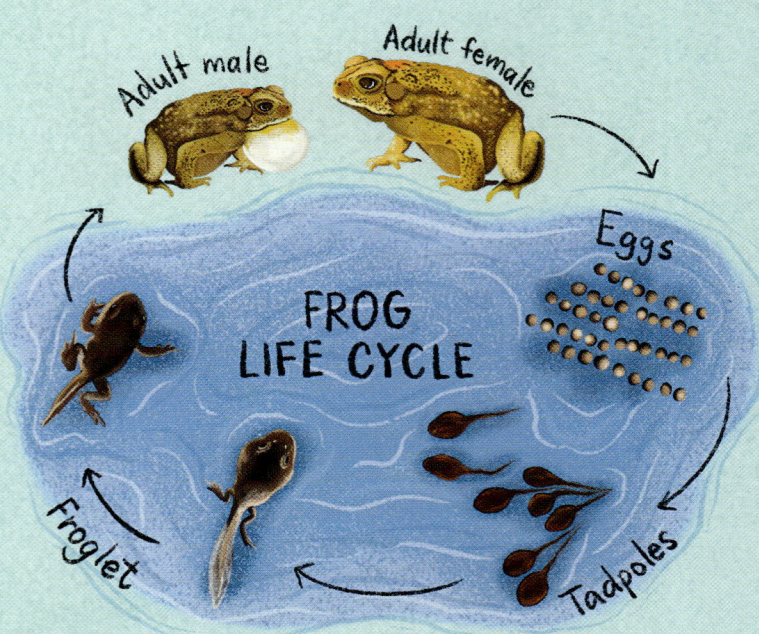

A watery romance

Since tadpoles can only survive underwater, frogs do their best to ensure that their babies have plenty of water to swim in. They lay their eggs during rainy weather, when streams, ponds or natural pools are as full as can be. Male frogs gather near these water bodies and try their best to attract females. Most males are accomplished singers and croak a loud love song for their mates. The Indian Bullfrog turns bright yellow during this season to stand out, while the dancing frogs of the Western Ghats wave their hind legs for attention. The female frog lays her eggs in the water, and these soon hatch into tiny tadpoles.

Small Gliding Frog with her eggs

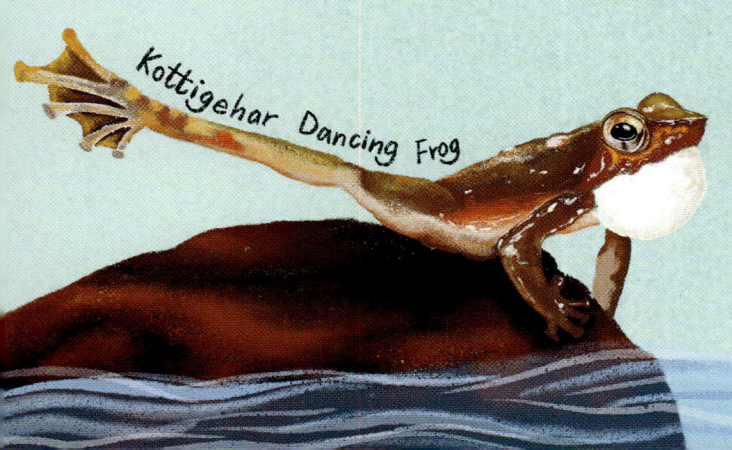

Kottigehar Dancing Frog

Not all frogs lay their eggs right into the water. In the southern parts of the Western Ghats, there are many kinds of frogs who lay their eggs on leaves! The frogs carefully choose leaves that hang over water. They then produce a sticky, foamy blanket that keeps the eggs moist. As the tadpoles hatch, they slip into the water below and are ready to start their lives.

Hidden from the heat and cold

Some animals, like those with fur or feathers, can maintain a constant body temperature in hot and cold weather. Other animals, like insects, snakes, turtles and amphibians like frogs, have a body temperature that changes with the temperature outside. This means that, depending on the weather, they can get very hot or very cold, and this is not always a good thing. Frogs have figured out a simple way to avoid extreme heat and cold: they hide! In hot, dry weather, they take shelter in wet soil, drains and other moist places to stay cool and hydrated. In winter, they burrow underground to avoid the cold. Finally, when it rains, they come out to celebrate the perfect weather and sing to each other!

You will need

- A plastic glass or container
- A pair of scissors
- A glass of water
- A rubber band (as thick as possible)
- A paper clip or small stick

> A frog with bumpy, warty skin is called a **toad**.

1. Turn the container upside down and mark the centre of the base. Ask an adult to help you make a small hole at the point you have marked.

2. Cut the rubber band and push one end through the hole so that it hangs inside the container. Tie the other end firmly to the paper clip or stick.

3. Pick up the container and hold it with one hand. Pull the long end of the rubber band straight, holding it tightly in your fingers.

4. Wet your thumb with water and stroke the rubber band firmly.

5. Now you are ready to join the frog concert! Experiment with different sizes of cups and rubber bands to make different croaking sounds!

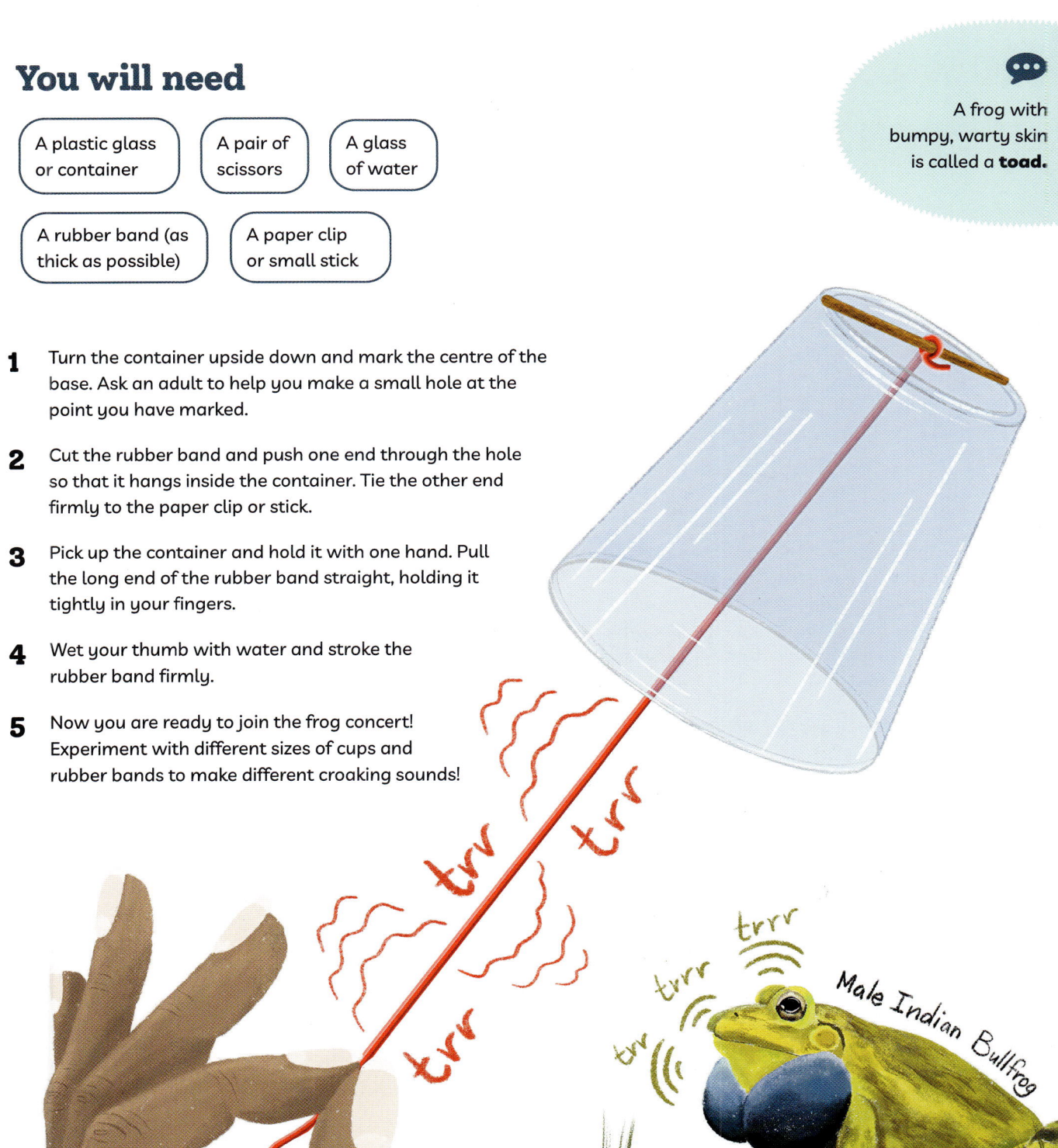

Male Indian Bullfrog

Have you ever seen a plant growing in a vase of water and wondered:

How do some plants grow without soil?

Whether in small table-top pots or vast forests, plants flourish in soil. Their roots burrow deep into the soil, sucking up water and nutrients. Even plants that grow underwater anchor themselves to the ground. But are there plants that can grow without soil?

You will need

- A paper and pencil

1. Starting inside your home, look for plants that grow without soil. They could be in water, among pebbles, growing from cracks in walls or even on other plants! Look out for greenery in unexpected places, or leaves that don't match a tree you're observing.

2. Make a list of where you find plants that are growing without soil.

3. Take a closer look at some of the plants around you – can you see the roots? What are they attached to? You can remove the plant and examine it carefully – just remember to plant it in soil when you are done!

How do you think those plants get water and nutrition?

....
....
....
....
....

How do you think the seeds of the plant reach the spot where it is growing?

....
....
....
....
....
....

Some plants grow on the trunks and branches of other plants. They use their host plants only for physical support and make their own food through photosynthesis. These are called **epiphytes**.

Plants in water

You may have observed some indoor plants like Money Plants or Lucky Bamboos growing in vases or bottles of water. Apart from water, where do you think they get the other nutrients needed to make food? Using their fine roots, these plants can absorb dissolved salts and minerals in tap water. However, since soil is much richer in nutrients, they grow faster and healthier if they are planted in a pot. You can try growing a cutting of Money Plant in soil and another in water, and compare the two.

Plants on other plants

Some leaves not matching the others on a tree? You could be looking at an epiphyte. They can be tiny, like mosses; bushy, like ferns; or huge, like fig trees. They depend on moisture from the air or rain, and gain nutrients from fallen leaves, dust and other particles stuck among branches.

Plants on walls

On taking a closer look at walls and terraces, you may see green patches or tiny seedlings growing from cracks. Creepers like bougainvillea and morning glory often grow vertically using walls as support, but their roots are firmly in the soil. However, some plants like mosses, ficuses and grasses can grow using only the little dust and soil particles trapped in the crevices in walls and other human-built structures. Water from rain or mist seeps into the crevices, helping the plant make food. As it grows, a plant's roots expand and split the crack further, making more space to trap dust and water. Some figs grow roots until they reach the ground, and embed themselves in the soil below.

Traveling seeds

So now we know that some plants can grow in places without soil. But how do they reach these spots? Indoor plants are, of course, planted and nurtured by humans. Some plants like figs rely on animals to disperse their seeds through poop. If the poop lands in a sheltered crevice in a wall or tree trunk, the seeds have a safe place to grow. Others, like ferns and mosses, have tiny seeds and spores that travel with the wind and land on buildings and tree branches.

🔍 *Do seeds travel in other ways? Find out on **page 76**.*

Have you ever watched a fish in an aquarium and wondered:

How do animals breathe underwater?

Wherever there is water, there is life! At sub-zero temperatures and in hot water springs, in the fastest-flowing rivers and the saltiest seas, millions of creatures live and breathe underwater. But how do they do this?

You will need

- A small metal pan
- A cup of water
- A stove

1. Pour the water into the metal pan. With an adult present, light the stove and place the pan on it. As the water begins to heat up, observe where the water touches the bottom of the pan – do you see something that wasn't there before?

2. Once the water starts boiling, switch off the stove.

✎ What changes did you notice when the water was heating?

....
....
....
....
....

Garden pond

Green algae

Air dissolving into water

What's in water?

Most plants and animals (including you!) breathe oxygen, a gas found in air. But there is also oxygen in water! When you heated the water, you may have noticed small bubbles forming on the inner sides of the pan. These bubbles contain air that was mixed into or dissolved in the water. As water heats, the air dissolved in it separates out and forms tiny bubbles. These are different from the larger bubbles that form on the surface of water as it boils. You can try the same experiment with water from different sources – a nearby lake, aquarium or drinking water.

Plants releasing oxygen

During the activity, you saw that as water heats up, tiny bubbles of air containing dissolved oxygen form. As the water gets warmer, more and more bubbles are released into the air. This means that there is less dissolved oxygen left in the water. As global temperatures rise, lakes, rivers and oceans are losing dissolved oxygen, which is a problem for the creatures that live in them.

How is there oxygen in water?

When air meets the surface of water, some of it mixes into the water. This dissolved air contains oxygen, which is what aquatic creatures breathe! Aquatic plants that live underwater or have leaves floating on the surface also create dissolved oxygen. Like land plants, they make their food through photosynthesis. During this process, they release oxygen, which then dissolves in the water.

Aquatic organisms called algae also make their food through photosynthesis, releasing oxygen into water. Some algae look a little bit like plants, but they don't have roots or flowers. Others can only be seen with a magnifying glass or microscope.

Goldfish

Animals underwater

Fish and some aquatic snails have special organs called gills that allow them to breathe the oxygen underwater. Amphibians like frogs and the larvae of some insects like dragonflies absorb oxygen through their skin.

Not all aquatic animals can breathe underwater! Unlike fish, whales and dolphins are mammals and don't have gills. They can hold their breath underwater for a long time, and come up to the surface every few hours to take a huge gulp of air.

Skittering Frog

🔍 Remember 'photosynthesis'? Refresh your memory on **page 18**.

Apple Snail

💬 Plants and animals that live in water are known as **aquatic organisms**.

Have you ever picked up a scent and wondered:

Do smells have meanings?

Animals and plants don't need words to communicate with each other. Apart from vivid colours and a variety of sounds, they also interact with their surroundings through smells!

You will need
- A paper and pencil

Let your nose lead you on an exploration of your home and surroundings. Try to find as many of the smells in this checklist as possible. When you find a smell that fits, write it down and move to the next one.

- ☐ An earthy smell
- ☐ A smell that you want to keep smelling
- ☐ A smell that reminds you of something
- ☐ An unexpectedly good smell
- ☐ Something you smell everyday
- ☐ A smell that makes you happy
- ☐ A smell that you never want to smell again!
- ☐ A smell you like, but someone else doesn't
- ☐ A smell you haven't smelt before

Smelly memories

Did you notice how the smells around you can evoke memories and emotions? The parts of our brain that process smells are also responsible for processing emotions and memories. This is why a smell can often transport us back in time to a specific moment or place, or make us feel a certain way. For example, the smell of your favourite food may remind you of your family, and make you feel happy and relaxed.

Animals and plants use special scents called **pheromones** to communicate messages to others of their own kind.

Scientists who study smell encourage us to pay attention to the smells around us. This helps to strengthen our sense of smell and gives us another way to interact with our surroundings!

Smelly conversations

Humans can recognise thousands of different smells, but some animals can have entire conversations through their noses! Dogs often investigate each other by sniffing each other's faces and backsides, and they can use this information to decide if they want to be friends or not. A single sniff can tell a dog a lot about another dog – its health, mood, where it has been and what it has eaten. In fact, dogs and many other animals can recognise each other based on smell alone. It would probably take humans many conversations to learn as much about each other as dogs do with a single sniff!

🔍 *How else do animals leave smelly messages for each other? Find out on **page 74**.*

Smelly messages

Have you ever sent a note to a friend in a secret language? Animals and plants do it, too – through pheromones! They can give off specific scents to send messages to each other.

When female spiders want to mate, they leave a trail of silk with pheromones that tells males where to find them.

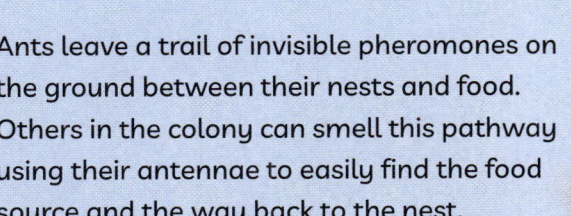

Ants leave a trail of invisible pheromones on the ground between their nests and food. Others in the colony can smell this pathway using their antennae to easily find the food source and the way back to the nest.

Some plants release alarm pheromones when they are being eaten by herbivores. The other plants can sense this signal through their leaves and begin to release chemicals that can make the herbivore sick. The hungry herbivore then has to look for a meal somewhere else!

Have you ever seen a caterpillar feasting a leaf and wondered:

How do plants protect themselves?

They can't run away or chase off potential predators, but they are the favourite food of many animals, big and small. Animals who eat plants are called herbivores and range from huge elephants to tiny ants. So how do plants protect themselves from becoming breakfast, lunch and dinner?

Lime Swallowtail caterpillar

You will need

- 1 small piece of ripe banana/papaya or any other sweet fruit, without the peel
- A tablespoon of a herb like mint, tulsi or lemongrass, crushed into a paste
- A watch or mobile phone to keep time

1. Keep the fruit and herb paste in different dishes.
2. Just before sunset, step outdoors. Insects, especially flying insects such as moths and mosquitos, are very active during this time.
3. Place the dishes around 2-arms-distance apart, in a place where you can see flying insects.
4. Observe the dishes for 15 minutes and note down any insect activity around the food.
5. Next, add the herb paste into the dish with the fruit, and observe what happens.

✏️ Which dish attracted more insects, the one with the herb paste or the one with the fruit?

....
....
....
....

✏️ Why do you think insect activity on the 2 kinds of food was different?

....
....
....
....
....
....
....
....
....
....
....
....

Common Evening Brown

💬 Scientists who study plants are called **botanists**.

Eww ... what smells?

Some plants, like mint, tulsi or marigold, smell delightful to our human noses – but to insects, they stink! While observing the insects, you may have noticed that they were not as interested in the herb paste as they were in the fruit – some may even have abandoned the delicious fruit because the herb smelled so bad to them. Some plants protect themselves from herbivores through strong-smelling leaves and stems. Check the label of a mosquito repelling cream or spray – you may see 'lemongrass' or 'citronella' listed in the ingredients. These ingredients, as well as other plants that smell like lemon, make insects fly away in the opposite direction. Other plants like milkweeds and Oleander are full of white sap that is toxic to herbivores.

Ouch! That plant just poked me!

Plants also protect themselves from hungry herbivores by growing strong, tough barks and sharp spines. To protect themselves from big herbivores like goats and cows, some trees, like the Acacias, have strong pointed thorns that can be more than 10 cm long. Have you seen the tiny curved thorns on rose plants? To discourage smaller herbivores like caterpillars and grasshoppers, some plants have very tiny, hair-like fibres called trichomes on the leaves and stems. The Mimosa or Touch-me-not Plant is sensitive to contact – when it is touched, its leaves close to protect themselves.

I get by with a little help from my friends

Some plants have struck up a deal with certain insects – 'You can live among my branches if you protect me!' Brown's Humboldtia, a flowering plant found in Southern India, has a modified stem for insects like ants and earthworms to live in. The ants are grateful for a safe home, and will protect the plant from animals that want to eat it.

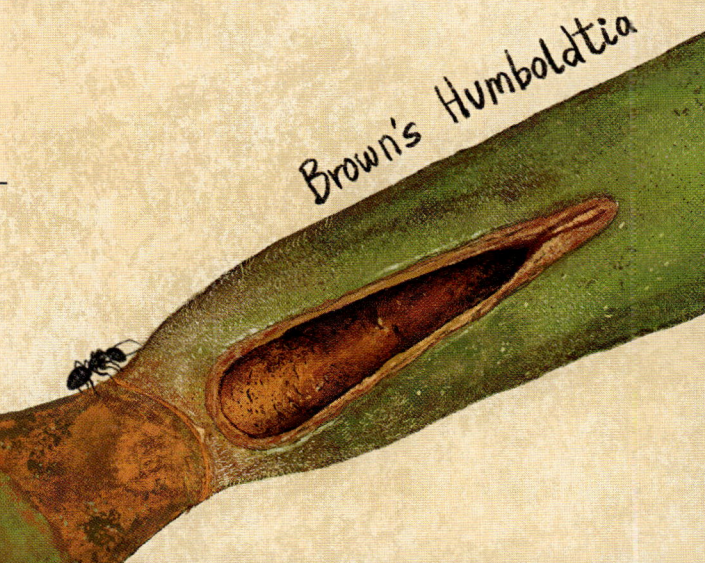

Have you ever seen a bouquet of flowers and wondered:

Why do flowers look so different from each other?

Bees, butterflies, birds and bats have something in common – they are a plant's best friend! These creatures visit flowers in search of delicious sweet nectar, and plants rely on them to carry pollen to other flowers of the same kind. Once the pollen reaches the other flower, it starts off an amazing reaction. The flower gets fertilised, and grows a fruit. And if the seeds from the fruit find a comfortable place, they grow into new plants! But if all these flowers want to invite animals, why don't they all look similar?

You will need

- 4 small, shallow transparent containers (like cut plastic bottles)
- Coloured paper – blue, yellow, white and green
- Sugar
- Water
- A pair of scissors
- A watch or mobile phone to keep time

1. Find an outdoor space where you can sit and observe some plants. The best time to do this activity is just after sunrise or just before sunset, when insects are very active.

2. Using a pencil, draw a flower shape on one of the pieces of paper. The flower should be roughly as wide as your open hand. Cut out the flower. Trace the shape onto another piece of paper and cut. Do this until you have identical flowers in all 4 colours.

3. Dissolve 2 tablespoons of sugar into 4 tablespoons of water.

4. Place your paper flowers on flat ground, at least 5 steps away from each other. If it's a windy day, you can weigh them down using small stones.

5. Pour the sugar syrup into the transparent containers. Place one container at the centre of each paper flower.

6. Observe your flowers for half an hour and note down insect activity.

✏️ Did any one of your flowers attract more insects than the others? Which insects?

....
....
....
....

✏️ Did any one flower have very few or no visitors?

....
....

✏️ Why do you think this happened?

....
....
....
....
....
....

Colour

All flowering plants want to form seeds so that their seeds can go on to grow into new plants. They use their shape, size, colour and smell to invite a pollinator's attention. Flowers come in bright colours to stand out among green leaves. Did you notice if any one of your flowers attracted more of one type of insect than others? Insects see colours differently from humans, and some insects like one colour better than another. For example, bees are attracted to blue and violet. Some insects like colours where they can blend in and hide from predators while they eat. For example, yellow butterflies have been observed to prefer yellow flowers.

Shape

The shape of a flower is designed to attract particular pollinators. Some flowers are open or bowl-shaped, with lots of space to sit – inviting a variety of tired and hungry insect pollinators. Others are shaped like tubes with the nectar at the end – inviting animals with long, thin mouthparts, like a bird's beak or a butterfly's proboscis. The pollen in a flower is cleverly positioned so that when an animal tries to reach the nectar, it ends up pollinating the flower.

Male Green-tailed Sunbird and Marmalade Bush

> When pollen grains are carried from one flower to another, it is called **pollination**. Animals that help plants with pollination are called **pollinators.**

Rafflesia flower

Size

Many flowers like lilies and lotuses are large in size so that they are more visible to passing pollinators. The Rafflesia flower is found in the rainforests of Sumatra and Borneo, and can grow up to 3 feet across!

Smell

Many pollinators use smell to track down flowers. Some pollinators like bees, butterflies and bats are particularly attracted to sweet-smelling flowers. Bats can find strong-scented Mahua flowers in the dark using only their sense of smell.

Flies and beetles are often attracted to rotting smells – and so, plants like Rafflesia have stinky flowers to attract them!

Short-nosed Fruit Bat

Mahua flower

Have you ever gazed into the eyes of a butterfly and wondered:

How do insects see the world?

Bees, butterflies and flies can see the smallest of flowers from a distance, and dragonflies can spot and capture mosquitos in mid-air. You creep up slowly from behind, but that pesky housefly always seems to see you just in time to get away. So how do flies and other insects see the world around them?

You will need

- A spherical object that fits comfortably in your hand, like a ball or an orange
- A piece of aluminium foil without any wrinkles, big enough to wrap around the spherical object
- A small mirror
- A bright-coloured A4 size paper
- A sketch pen or crayon
- A pair of scissors
- Glue

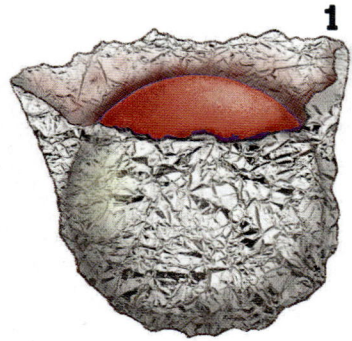

1. With your hands, scrunch the foil lightly. Wrap the foil around the spherical object, with its shinier side facing out.

2. Cut the paper into 2 strips along the length. Glue the ends of the strips together to form 1 long strip.

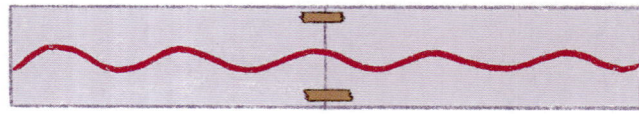

3. Along the whole strip, draw a bold pattern of your choice in bright colours.

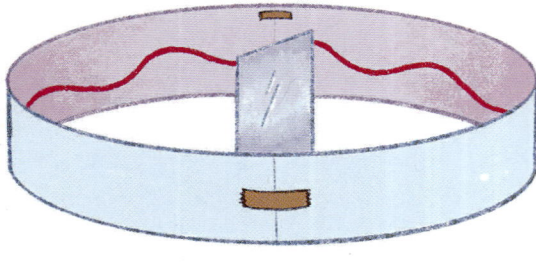

4. Join the 2 ends of the long strip to form a circle, with the pattern on the inside surface. Place the circle on a table or the floor.

5. Place the mirror in the centre of the circle, with the reflective side facing the inner surface of the paper. You can use something small and heavy to prop up the mirror, if needed.

6. Observe this from all sides. Note what sections of the circle are reflected in the mirror.

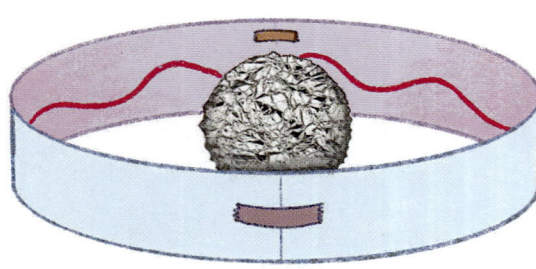

7. Now, remove the mirror and place the foil-covered sphere in the centre of the circle.

8. Observe the reflection of the inner side of the circle on the foil sphere. Note what you see.

✏️ Could you see the full inner surface of the circle on both reflective surfaces?

....
....
....

✏️ What were the differences between the 2 sets of reflections?

....
....
....

I see, you see, but what do they see?

Insects see the world very differently from us! You may have noticed that the mirror could only reflect a part of the circle – to reflect the other parts, you would have to move it around. This is similar to how humans and many other animals see the world. We have simple eyes, which can only see one image from one direction at a time. To look in a different direction, we have to turn our heads.

You may have noticed that the coloured side of the paper ring was reflected all around the foil ball, but the reflection was broken into little pieces due to the crushed foil. An insect's eye is similar. Insects have compound eyes, which are made up of hundreds of tiny eyes. Each tiny eye captures part of an image, and the insect's brain assembles them into a complete picture. Like the foil ball, the compound eye can take in images from multiple directions at once, allowing insects to see in front, behind and to the side without turning their heads.

A flower seen through a simple eye

Nectar guide

A flower seen through a compound eye

A cat

A bee

Through their compound eyes, insects can see ultraviolet light – a group of colours that humans can't see at all! This helps them see patterns in flowers, invisible to the human eye, called nectar guides. These bold patterns lead insects to the flower's nectar, saying – 'Here's your next meal, and only you can see it!'

Flying insects like dragonflies have excellent vision. This helps them to move around without bumping into anything, and to spot and catch their food in mid-air. The eyes of dragonflies take up almost all the space on their heads, and each compound eye has 30,000 tiny simple eyes. Some insects, like ants, can only make out shapes, and use light and shadow to guide their path. Others, like wasps, can see and remember human faces, so treat them kindly!

Insects' compound eyes are made up of thousands of tiny eye-lenses called **ommatidia**.

Have you ever looked up at a towering Banyan and wondered:

Where are the flowers of fig trees?

The Ficus or fig family has around 850 types of trees, 89 of which can be found in India – including Banyan, Peepal and Gular (Cluster Fig). Most fig trees have similar looking fruits – rounded at the bottom and ending in a stem on top. Fig fruits can be of different sizes and all of them have a tiny hole at the bottom, which is sometimes too small to see with our eyes. Each fig tree can produce hundreds of these fruits, but we never end up seeing any visible flowers! An old folk tale tells us that the flowers of the Gular tree can only be found by those with good fortune. In a way, this legend is true!

 Although some types of fig fruits are edible for humans, most are best left for birds and insects. Do not eat wild figs!

🔍 *How do flowers form fruits? Refresh your memory on **page 40**.*

You will need

- Sheets of paper for drawing
- A pencil
- Crayons, colour pencils or any colouring material of your choice
- A knife

1. With the help of an adult, search for a fig tree nearby. You may find one growing from the ground, wrapped around another tree, or growing out of a crack in an old wall or building.

2. Observe the tree closely. Do you see fruits? Where are they growing? Do you see flowers? Do you see animals, big or small, in the tree?

3. Collect some fruits from the tree – you may find fruits on the ground under the tree, or growing on the trunk and near the leaves.

4. Find a comfortable place to sit near the tree. Observe the fruits very carefully – do you see any holes on their skins or at the bottom? Make a detailed drawing of a fruit.

5. With the help of an adult, slice open a fig fruit. Observe it carefully and make a detailed drawing of what you see.

✏️ Without flowers, how do you think the fig tree forms fruits?

....
....
....
....

✏️ Why do you think all fig fruits have a hole at the bottom?

....
....
....
....

Friend of the fruit

If you cut open an unripe green fig fruit, you may notice tiny bulbs on the inside surface. The young, green 'fruits' of the fig tree are actually clusters of flowers! Each tiny bulb in the fruit is an individual flower which will develop into a seed. But how does pollination take place if they are sealed inside the fig fruit? With the help of the only creature that can find the fig flower – the fig wasp! These tiny wasps are the only animals that can pollinate fig flowers, and the inside of the fig is the perfect nursery for their eggs.

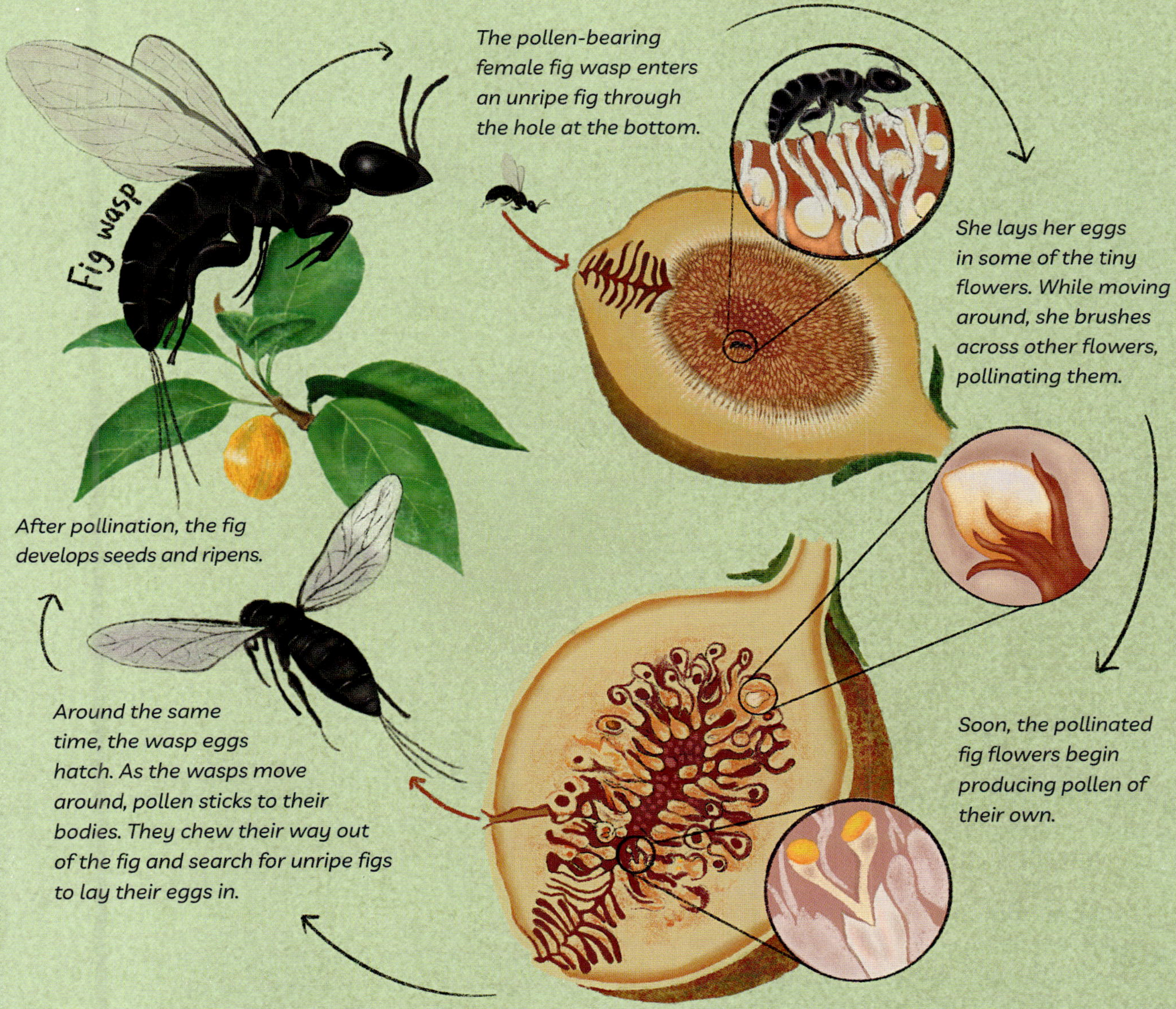

The pollen-bearing female fig wasp enters an unripe fig through the hole at the bottom.

She lays her eggs in some of the tiny flowers. While moving around, she brushes across other flowers, pollinating them.

After pollination, the fig develops seeds and ripens.

Soon, the pollinated fig flowers begin producing pollen of their own.

Around the same time, the wasp eggs hatch. As the wasps move around, pollen sticks to their bodies. They chew their way out of the fig and search for unripe figs to lay their eggs in.

Favourite of the furry and feathered

Figs and fig wasps depend closely on each other, but there are more characters in this story! Other insects, birds and mammals love the taste of fig fruits. Thanks to the fig wasp, a ripe fruit contains thousands of seeds, each ready to grow into a tree. Birds and mammals digest the sweet, nutritious part of the fig, and poop out the seeds. If the seeds land in a suitable place, they will go on to grow into majestic trees.

In nature, living beings often form partnerships that benefit from each other. Th s is called **mutualism**.

Have you ever scratched your head and wondered:

Why do lice like living on our heads?

Most people get lice at least once in their lives! But with a whole world out there, why do lice like living on our heads? Are there other animals like lice?

1. Start by speaking to someone who lives with a dog, cat, bird or any other animal. Ask them if they have ever found tiny creatures living on their pet's body. Request that they show you pictures, sketches, or even the creatures themselves.

2. Ask adults who live with you – have they ever found insects or small creatures living on your body?

3. Make a list of all these tiny creatures!

Creature	Where it lives
1	
2	
3	
4	
5	
6	
7	
8	

Why do you think they choose to live on other animals?

....
....
....
....

A **parasite** is an organism that depends on another living being, known as its **host**, for food and survival. Parasites live on or inside the bodies of their hosts.

> Lice, ticks and fleas can cause us discomfort through itchy and sometimes painful bites. Wash your hands well after playing with animals!

It's all about survival!

All living things aim to stay safe, healthy, and to reproduce. They spend their days searching for food, shelter and keeping themselves out of harm's way. But some creatures have figured out a shortcut – why not let someone else do all the work?

Cunning creatures

Parasites are incredibly clever! They choose hosts that are many times larger than themselves, and take just enough food from a host's body so that the host remains healthy and comfortable. This way, the parasites get a steady supply of food, and their hosts either don't notice the parasites or decide that it's too much work to remove them. For example, humans (including you!) have tiny mites living in our eyebrows. They help us stay clean by eating dead skin and are so small that you would need a microscope to see them!

Other parasites like ticks, lice and fleas are more noticeable. They live on the skin of animals, especially those with hair or fur, and feed on blood through itchy or painful bites. In case the host notices and tries to remove them, these parasites are well prepared! They have specialised body parts like suckers or hooked mouths, and flat bodies so that they can hide against the skin of their hosts and move away quickly among the hair.

🔍 Why do plants need leaves to make food? More on **page 16**.

Smarty-plants

Plants can be parasitic too! They have specialised body parts that latch onto another plant's stem to steal nutrition and water. Mistletoe and Cuscuta are common parasites that use other plants as hosts. Cuscuta (called Amarbel in Hindi) plants are completely dependent on their host for food. Since they don't make their own food, they don't need to have leaves! If you see a tree or bush covered in what looks like yellow noodles, you've spotted a Cuscuta plant!

Have you ever found a potato with sprouts and wondered:

Do all plants come from seeds?

Plants are found everywhere, from the deepest forests to our own kitchens, and they all have a common goal – to keep on growing and increasing their numbers! Plants have developed various ways of multiplying. If you have grown plants, you know that one of the ways to do it is by planting seeds. But can you grow a plant without sowing a seed? Let's find out.

Potato

You will need

- A few sprigs of mint/basil/tulsi at least 15 cm long, without the roots
- A transparent glass or bottle
- Water

1. Remove the leaves from the lower part of each mint sprig, leaving at least 4 inches of bare stem.
2. Place the sprigs in a glass with the stems downwards, and fill the glass with water.
3. Make daily observations for 7 days, and note the changes each day.

Did the stem or leaves change in any way?

....
....
....
....
....

If you see small roots growing, where do you think they came from?

....
....
....
....
....
....

💬 A scientist who studies trees and plants is called a **botanist**. Some botanists study **propagation**, which is the process of how plants grow and multiply.

Growing a plant from a plant

You may have noticed that your mint stems grew fresh roots after a few days of being kept in water. From just a handful of stems, you grew new plants! If they are planted in soil, they will keep growing, even though they didn't come from a seed. Like the mint plant, many plants can grow from part of a stem, root or leaf. This would be like a full human growing from a hair or tooth! The part of a plant used to grow a new plant is often called a cutting. Visit a local nursery or ask someone who loves gardening which plants they grow from cuttings.

An amazing ability

You may have seen how grass cut short at the base grows back in a few weeks, or fresh shoots sprout at the base of a cut tree. The ability of plants to grow leaves, stems and roots from just one part of their body helps them in many ways. This means that plants can heal their injuries, regrow lost parts and keep growing throughout their lives! This ability also helps us propagate plants for food, gardening and forestry, too.

Mint, garlic, ginger, potato, bamboo, banana and many other edible plants can grow if we plant just a piece of the stem.

Some plants, like succulents, can grow from a single leaf! Bryophyllum plants produce hundreds of tiny plants along the edges of their leaves. These plantlets soon fall to the ground and take root in the soil.

Mangrove forests protect the coasts of India and can be grown by planting pieces of the stem of a parent plant. The planted stem soon forms roots and leaves, and eventually grows into a tree.

Have you ever heard a symphony of birdsong and wondered:

Which bird is singing?

Sometimes, we are awoken by the dawn chorus – several birds singing at the top of their voices. But how do we match the song to the bird? Folk tales can give us a clue.

The cuckoo family of birds has inspired many stories across India. The males sing unique and distinctive songs to attract females or keep rivals away. The Common Hawk-Cuckoo is also called the Brainfever Bird. Its three syllable song sounds like someone yelling 'Brain FE-ver! Brain FE-ver!' louder and louder. It even has a mad look in its eyes to match! British naturalists noted that it sounds like a complaint about the heat, since the male starts calling at the beginning of summer. In Tamil, it is called *Akka Kuyil* (*'kuyil'* being a general word for birds of the cuckoo family). This is based on the folk story of two sisters bathing in a river, when the elder sister was washed away by the current. The Common Hawk-Cuckoo sounds like the younger sister calling for her *akka*, which means elder sister in Tamil. In Bengali, it says *'Chokh gelo!'*, which means 'My eyes are gone!'. In Maharashtra, the bird is the bringer of good news, calling *'Paos ala!'* – rain is coming!

Up in the Himalayas, the Indian Cuckoo is considered a prankster. It was summer in the mountains and a young boy and his mother had just picked a basketful of ripe *kaphal*, or box myrtle fruit. The mother left her son to guard the basket, but when she returned, the fruit was gone! The culprit was an Indian Cuckoo, but when asked if he did it, he sang his musical call which sounds like *'Kaphal pakyo, mai na chakyo!'* In Kumaoni, this means 'I haven't even tasted the ripe kaphal!' In nature, some species of cuckoos are pranksters in a very different way – they lay an egg in another bird's nest, tricking the foster parents into raising the chick!

In Uttarakhand, the Common Cuckoo is locally known as *Kuppu Katthi*. It is a migratory bird and arrives at the same time as the red Rhododendron flowers begin to bloom. In Kumaoni, the Rhododendron is known as *'Kuppu'* and the word *'Katthi'* means beautiful. The bird's repetitive call sounds like it is flying around and informing everyone that the beautiful flowers are in bloom.

> Ornithologists and bird enthusiasts often use stories or a pattern of words or letters to help them remember bird calls. This type of memory technique is called a **mnemonic**.

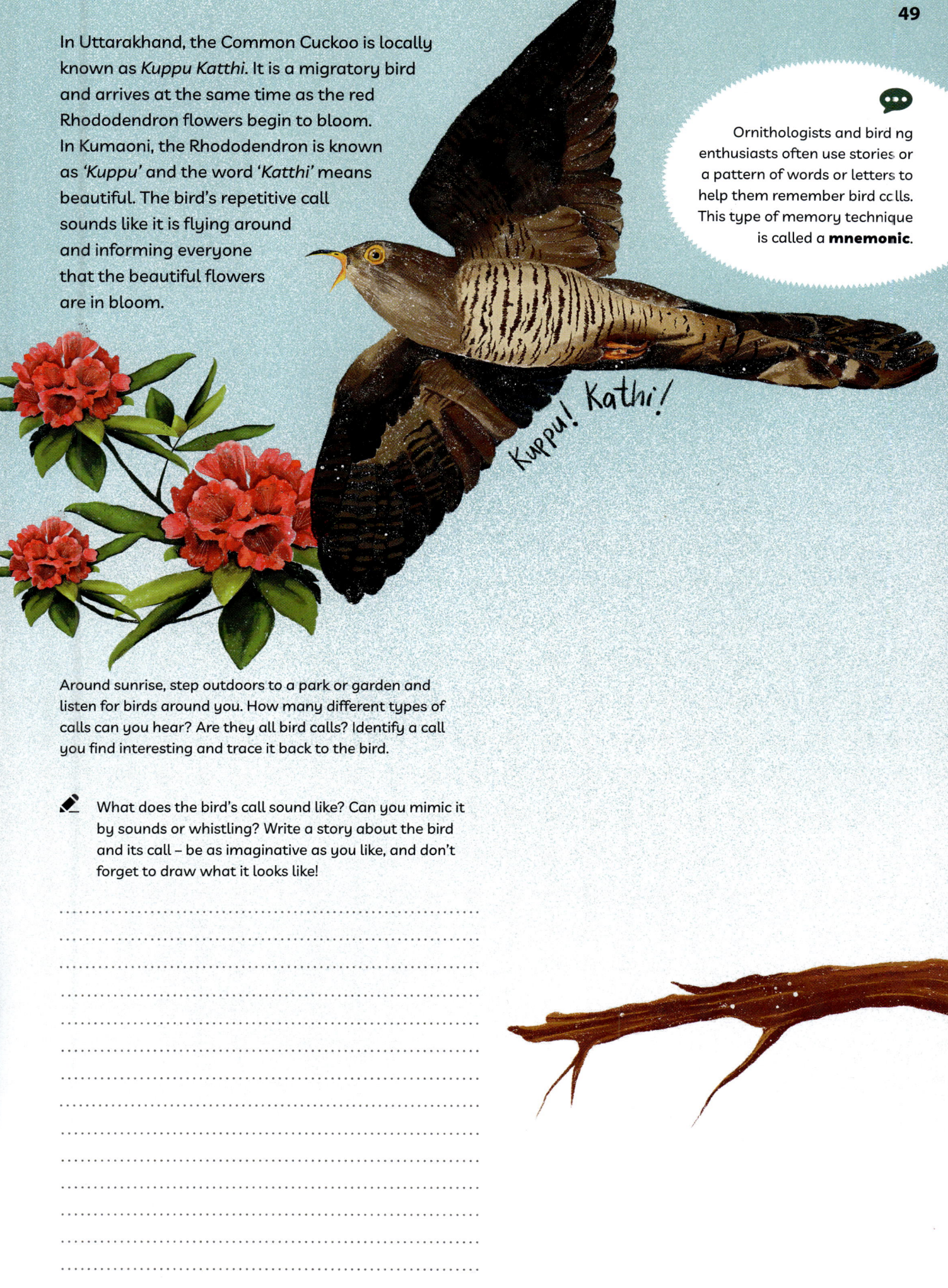

Kuppu! Kathi!

Around sunrise, step outdoors to a park or garden and listen for birds around you. How many different types of calls can you hear? Are they all bird calls? Identify a call you find interesting and trace it back to the bird.

✎ What does the bird's call sound like? Can you mimic it by sounds or whistling? Write a story about the bird and its call – be as imaginative as you like, and don't forget to draw what it looks like!

....
....
....
....
....
....
....
....
....
....
....

A whistling pressure cooker, a cricket chirping, a motorbike passing by, are all sounds of life.

What does sound tell us about our surroundings?

Words and pictures are not the only ways of describing what's happening around us. Often, we may be able to hear something without seeing it – like the wind, a cricket hidden among the grass or a garbage collection truck in the neighbouring street. How does the soundscape vary in different places and times?

You will need

A watch or mobile phone to keep time

1 Choose a spot in your street or neighbourhood.

2 Visit it at 2 different times – once early in the morning and once in the afternoon.

3 During each visit, sit or stand in one place for 15 minutes. Write down all the sounds you hear – different kinds of vehicles, people talking, street vendors selling their wares, mosquitos buzzing, birds calling, dogs barking, and other sounds that reach you.

4 Categorise the sounds into different types – physical sounds (like the wind blowing or water flowing), biological sounds (made by all kinds of creatures) and human-related sounds (vehicles, pressure cookers, people talking etc).

If you hear a sound you don't recognise, try to mimic or record it and ask friends and family to help you identify it. If possible, you can also follow the sound to its source. You can also do this activity in different places, like a park and a roadside, and compare the results.

Time	Physical sounds	Biological sounds	Human-related sounds

✎ Were the types of sounds you heard in the morning and afternoon different? How so?

✎ Were there some sounds you heard only during one time of the day?

✎ Were there sounds you couldn't identify or see the source of?

Changing soundscapes

You may notice that the kinds of sounds you hear change with time and place. The same place can sound completely different at different times of the day. If you visit very early in the morning, you may hear the dawn chorus – when birds sing at the start of the day. The afternoon may be more silent, since animals may take shelter to avoid the heat. Did you notice this sort of a pattern in your observations? Similarly, as a place changes, its soundscape changes. For example, when the number of cars in a place increases, traffic sounds can drown out the calls of birds, frogs and squirrels. Scientists have also found that spending time in nature and listening to natural sounds helps people feel calmer and more relaxed – so, whether it's early in the morning or away from human-related hustle and bustle, be sure to get a dose of nature when you can!

City sounds affect wild animals, too. Scientists have found that in areas with more traffic, some birds start calling more loudly – they have to shout to be heard over the increased volume of sounds in their surroundings. Sometimes, these birds alter their calls so much that they end up sounding quite different from birds of their own kind living in forests.

Sound all around

Listening to the soundscapes of your neighbourhood can tell you about the types of birds, insects and other animals you can find there. Following a sound to its source can help you learn more about the animal making the sound – where it lives and how it behaves. Even if you can't see the animal, you can learn what time it likes to come out. For example, traffic sounds in the morning tell us when humans like to come out in their cars, buses or autorickshaws, to go to school and work. Other animals also have their own daily activities. Many birds are the most active at dawn but others, like kites, come out after sunrise. Others still are the most active at night, like owls.

So, even if you are indoors, or out at night in the dark, listening to sounds can give you clues that the eyes may not be able to see!

Scientists record and study soundscapes of spaces to understand more about humans and other animals there. This field of science is called **bioacoustics**.

On seeing a brightly coloured butterfly, have you ever wondered:

Why are some animals so colourful?

Animals come in varying shades and patterns, spots and stripes, and sometimes, all of these together. It is no wonder that artists are inspired by nature! But is there a reason behind these bold colours and patterns?

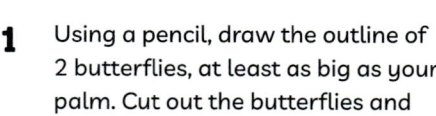

You will need: White paper | A pencil and eraser | A pair of scissors | Crayons, colour pencils or paints | A watch or mobile phone to keep time

1. Using a pencil, draw the outline of 2 butterflies, at least as big as your palm. Cut out the butterflies and erase the outline.

2. Find a room in which you can conduct this activity. Your goal is to hide one butterfly while keeping it in plain sight (not under or behind something). This is your 'Bashful Butterfly'. The second butterfly – the 'Bold Butterfly' – has to stand out and be easy to spot.

3. Find a colourful or patterned surface in the room and colour your Bashful Butterfly to match the surface as closely as possible. Place the butterfly against the background.

4. Choose a different spot for your Bold Butterfly, and colour it so that it stands out and you can see it immediately.

5. Ask a parent, teacher or friend to find both butterflies and use a timer to see how long it takes them to find each one. You can also try it again with a different person or with differently coloured butterflies.

✏️ Which butterfly did they find first?
....
✏️ Why do you think this happened?
....
....
....

Hiding in plain sight

Animals use their colours and patterns to hide, or to make themselves easy to spot. Like your Bashful Butterfly, some animals camouflage themselves among leaves, tree bark, rocks, or just about any other surface in nature. Some, like the Common Baron butterfly caterpillar, are coloured exactly like their host plants to hide from predators like birds. Others, like a crab spider or a tiger crouching in long grass, blend in with their background so that they can sneak up and surprise their prey.

A camouflaged crab spider with its catch

Can you spot the Common Baron Butterfly caterpillar?

When animals use their colours and patterns to blend into the background and hide from others, it is called **camouflage**.

The Purple Sunbird displays yellow feathers during the mating season

If you eat me, you'll get a bad tummy so stay away!

Plain Tiger Butterfly

Look at me!

During your game, the Bold Butterfly was probably much easier to spot than the Bashful Butterfly because its colouration made it stand out. Some animals use their colours to draw attention to themselves. Birds like the peacock and Purple Sunbird use their brightly coloured feathers, sometimes paired with loud calls and dance moves, to attract mates.

Danger! Stay away from me!

You may have seen brightly coloured signs and posters saying 'NO PARKING' or 'ROAD CLOSED'. They are designed to be easily noticed. This tactic of using vibrant colours to catch attention is borrowed from nature. Poisonous or toxic animals often have striking colours and patterns to signal that they are dangerous to potential predators.

Has a moth ever flown by you at night and left you wondering:

Why do moths prefer darkness to daylight?

The night-flying cousins of butterflies remain something of a mystery to us – even though there are 10 times as many moth species as there are butterflies! While we sleep, moths flutter around our homes, gardens, forests and fields. But why do these creatures prefer the darkness, and what are they up to during the day?

You will need

- Paper and pencil
- A plain white wall outdoors, with a light source
- A torch
- You can also use a plain white bedsheet, clothesline and clothespins

Molly Monkey Moth

Footman moth

Large Milkweed Snout

1. On a dark, preferably moonless night, observe insect activity around the outdoor light. Alternatively, you can pin a white sheet onto a clothesline outdoors and position a torch so that the light shines onto the sheet. This is a do-it-yourself version of a 'light trap' or 'light sheet', a tool that moth researchers use to attract, observe and study moths. The best time to see moths is during the monsoons or after it has just rained. Ask an adult to accompany you!

2. Describe each moth that is attracted to your light sheet and note down the most striking identifying features. In addition, you can also use a camera or mobile phone to take pictures of the moths.

3. Observe your light sheet for at least an hour. After the hour is up, turn off the light.

4. The next morning, revisit the same place and try to find the same moths you saw. You can refer to your notes or pictures.

✎ Why do you think we asked you to do this activity on a moonless night?

....
....
....

✎ Were you able to find any of the moths you saw during the night?

....
....

> *
> Moths' wings and bodies are covered in tiny, soft scales which help them fly. These come off easily when touched. Avoid handling moths, especially their delicate wings!

Night-time navigators

Before this activity, you may not have noticed many moths around your home. This means that their plan is working! They prefer to come out under the cover of darkness while other animals are asleep – especially birds and other predators who see them as a meal. Moths are remarkable navigators, and map their way through the darkness using stars and moonlight. In urban spaces, they often get confused by artificial light sources and fly towards them instead. Their branched antennae are their noses, helping them sniff out flowers like jasmines and Parijata that bloom at night. Moths drink nectar from these flowers using a straw-like mouth, and also pollinate the flowers in this process.

> Animals that are active at night are called **nocturnal**.

Cocoa Tussock Moth caterpillar

Oleander Hawkmoth hidden among leaves

Common Crow Butterfly caterpillar

Disguised by day

As you might have noticed, moths are hard to spot during the day, unlike their cousins, the butterflies. In your observations, you may have seen beautiful, intricate markings on moths' wings. These delicate patterns help moths camouflage against natural surfaces like rocks, tree barks and leaves. However, moth babies (caterpillars) feed actively during the day. They can be spotted chomping on leaves, or in cupboards, feasting on grains and our favourite cotton clothes! When it is ready to pupate, a moth caterpillar weaves a cocoon around itself using thin, strong silk. A butterfly caterpillar, however, develops a hard coating called a chrysalis. Unlike butterflies, some moths also pupate underground.

🔍 *Why do moth caterpillars make a cocoon? Find out on **page 26**.*

Bat's breakfast?

While there are fewer predators out at night, that doesn't mean moths are safe. Moths are a favourite snack for bats. Insect-eating bats make high-pitched calls that echo off their prey, helping the bats locate their next meal. To defend themselves, some moths make sounds to inform bats that they are toxic, similar to how certain butterflies use bright colours as a warning. Other moths, like hawk moths, confuse bats by producing high-pitched clicks themselves!

Common Pipistrelle

Cyana moth emitting clicks to confuse a bat

Have you ever seen a slightly funny-looking bug and wondered:

Is that the animal I think it is?

Have you ever seen an ant with too many legs? Or heard a bird making an unexpected call? Animals are not always what they seem!

You will need

(This activity can be done with any 3 types of grains or pulses – 2 similar and 1 completely different.)

- 2 teaspoons whole moong dal (green)
- 2 teaspoons split toor/arhar dal (yellow)
- 2 teaspoons split chana dal (yellow)
- A shallow plate
- A stopwatch/mobile phone to keep time
- A partner to play with

1. For this activity, let's pretend you and your partner are birds. You both love green bugs (represented by the moong dal) and some yellow bugs (represented by the toor dal), but other types of yellow bugs (represented by the chana dal), are toxic, which means that eating them can make you fall sick. Take turns to play the game and see who can avoid the toxic yellow bugs!

2. Put all the grains of dal on the plate and mix them well. Then, spread them out evenly. Your goal is to pick out as many 'bugs' to eat as possible in 15 seconds and avoid getting sick. Using your thumb and finger like a beak, place the 'bugs' you have selected next to the plate.

3. Once the timer starts, pick out as many grains of moong and toor dal as you can, but try to avoid chana dal. In each round, one person can play the bird while the other person watches the timer.

4. Set the stopwatch to 15 seconds and start the timer.

5. Stop as soon as the timer reaches 15 seconds and count the number of safe bugs and toxic bugs you have picked. Switch sides and play again! Which bird managed to avoid falling sick?

✏️ Did you select more green bugs or yellow bugs?

....
....

✏️ Why did you choose more bugs of that particular colour?

....
....
....
....
....

💬 When an animal tricks prey or predators by pretending it is a different animal, it is called **mimicry**.

Visual trickery

While playing, you may have chosen more green bugs because you knew for sure that they were harmless. Meanwhile, since the safe yellow bugs and toxic yellow bugs look so much like each other, it may have been hard to select only the safe yellow bugs. It was probably easier to avoid all the yellow bugs so that you wouldn't fall sick. So, by being the same colour as the toxic yellow bugs, the safe yellow bugs avoided being eaten!

Let's look at another example. Many species of bees have a painful sting and warn predators about this by being brightly coloured. If you were a harmless fly, wouldn't you love to look like a bee so that you would be safe from danger? In nature, animals that are dangerous or toxic are sometimes very brightly coloured to warn predators away. Some non-toxic and perfectly yummy animals have learnt to take advantage of this system, and copy the behaviour, colours or smells of toxic animals in order to trick predators into staying away from them, too!

Red Weaver Ants have a painful bite and aggressively defend their colonies. It's no surprise that many animals like birds and wasps avoid eating them. A spider found in Southern India has evolved to look so much like the weaver ant that predators avoid the spider, too!

Which kind of bee has two wings instead of four?

A bee-mimicking drone fly!

🔍 *Why does the number of legs matter? More on **page 12**.*

Which is the ant and which is the spider?

Hint: Count the legs!

Sneaky sounds (and smells!)

Mimics use other kinds of trickery as well! Some clever spiders and wasps mimic how ants smell so that they can sneak into their nests and eat the ant larvae! Others, like the Racket-tailed Drongo, mimic the alarm calls of other birds while they are feeding. This is a special call that birds of the same species use to warn each other of danger. While the birds flee from the fake foe, the drongo swoops in and eats up whatever's left.

Have you seen a single bee buzzing around a flower and wondered:

Do all bees live in hives?

The bees we are most familiar with are called honeybees because – you guessed it – they make honey! Like ants, they live in large colonies (called hives) where each bee has a role. A single queen lays eggs which are fertilised by males (called drones), and female worker bees forage for food and build the hive. However, in other species, a single female bee forages, lays eggs and builds a nest for her young ones, all by herself!

Productive pollinators

At this moment, solitary bees may be visiting the flowering plants around you to collect nectar and pollen to feed themselves and their young. These bees are often metallic-looking and are typically hairier than their social cousins. The bristly hairs help the bee gather large amounts of pollen on her body, which she later dusts off in her nest. As the solitary bee travels from one flower to another, the loose pollen grains brush off on the flowers, pollinating them. This makes these bees very important and effective pollinators for many plants.

Carpenter bee visiting Giant Milkweed flower

Independent architects

Solitary bees lay their eggs in tube-like tunnels which they line with different materials. While some bees chew holes in wood and plant stems or dig holes in the ground, others find abandoned nests or cavities.

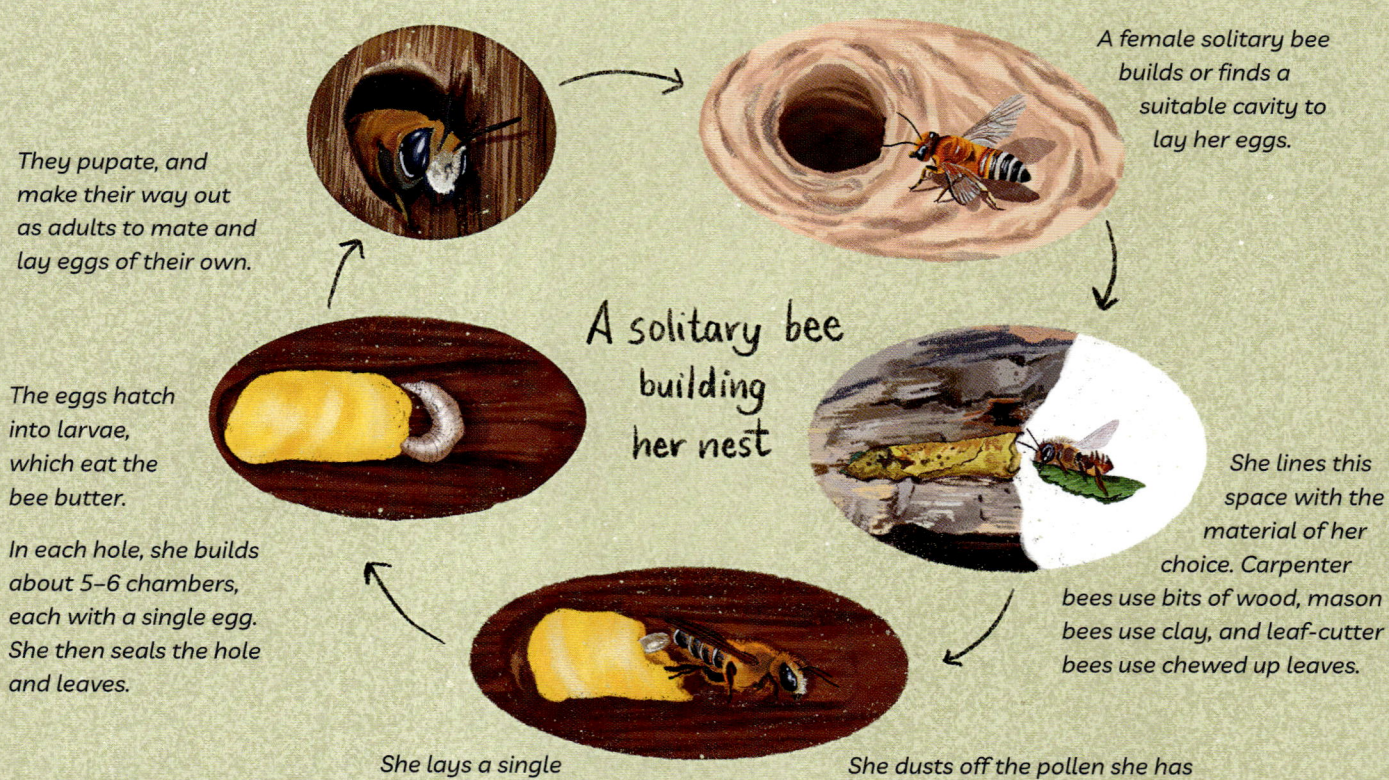

A solitary bee building her nest

A female solitary bee builds or finds a suitable cavity to lay her eggs.

She lines this space with the material of her choice. Carpenter bees use bits of wood, mason bees use clay, and leaf-cutter bees use chewed up leaves.

She dusts off the pollen she has collected and mixes it with nectar, making a paste called bee butter.

She lays a single egg and seals off the chamber.

In each hole, she builds about 5–6 chambers, each with a single egg. She then seals the hole and leaves.

The eggs hatch into larvae, which eat the bee butter.

They pupate, and make their way out as adults to mate and lay eggs of their own.

Unfortunately, solitary bees are finding fewer and fewer spaces to build their nests around us as natural spaces are replaced with buildings. But you can help these bees by creating a nesting space for them in your home, garden or school. Let's make a bee hotel!

You will need

- Different-sized sticks, bamboo straws or hollow stems. You can also use thick paper straws or tubes if bamboo isn't available.
- A clay or plastic flowerpot which is slightly taller than the straws
- A strong rope
- A pair of scissors

1. Cut or break the sticks to the same length as the straws.

2. Pack them tightly inside the flowerpot, making sure that they don't move around. Using sticks of different sizes will also create cavities in the gaps between them.

3. Find a sheltered place at least 5 feet high and near some flowering plants to keep your bee hotel. Turn it horizontally so that the sticks and straws are lying flat. Ask an adult to help you tie it to a fence, wall, tree trunk or some other base where it will remain undisturbed.

Species of bees in which the female lives independently throughout her life are known as **solitary bees.** Most species of bees are solitary, and build nests using leaves, wood and even clay!

To attract more bees, find out about what native flowering plants grow in your area, and try and plant some near your bee hotel. In hot weather, you can leave out a shallow dish of water with a few islands made from pebbles so that bees can sit and drink comfortably. You can also keep a potful of moist, sticky soil near your bee hotel for mason bees to use.

Have you ever seen a group of wasps guarding their lair and wondered:

What's inside a wasp nest?

Being a parent in the insect world is a tough job – you have to be a designer, architect, expert builder and hunter! You may have seen wasp nests without even knowing it – small paper-based hives hanging under a windowsill or an electrical socket plugged with mud. Wasps are the super-parents of the animal kingdom and build amazing nests to care for their young. But what's inside these nests and why do wasps guard them so fiercely?

Social or solitary

Wasps are one of the most diverse animal groups, and there are two broad types – those that live in colonies and those that don't.

Social wasps live in a group. Together, they build a nest using chewed-up plant fibres, with many hexagonal cells to house the eggs and larvae. Depending on the species, they may build a hanging nest in trees, under leaves, crevices in walls, under overhangs in buildings, or even underground.

Many species of wasps are solitary and don't build nests at all! Other solitary wasps make nests to house their own young. The female wasp builds a small nest using mud, or digs a burrow in the ground. Inside the nest, the wasp lays a few eggs. To make sure the larvae have a meal as soon as they hatch, she captures caterpillars, spiders and other bugs. Immobilising them with her sting, she carries them to her nest and seals them inside with her eggs.

The queen wasp lays an egg in each cell, which hatch into hungry larvae.

Social wasps

Polistes paper wasps

Female worker wasps guard the nest. They also catch caterpillars which they chew up to feed the larvae.

The fully grown larvae seal themselves inside their cells and metamorphose into adults to join the colony. Egg-laying females may also fly off to start their own colony.

Solitary wasp

Potter wasp

Inside the nest

> Wasps have strong mouthparts called **mandibles**. They use them to chew plant fibres into paper, capture and carry prey, and build their nests.

The wasp larvae hatch, and tuck into their pre-prepared meal. This gives them all the energy they need to metamorphose into adults, break open the nest and fly away.

Look around your home and neighbourhood to find the following types of wasp nests. When you see the nest, tick the box beside it. Watch carefully to see if the wasps are bringing back food for their larvae. Note if it is a social or solitary wasp nest.

Yellow Oriental Paper Wasp

☐ A small umbrella-shaped nest with many hexagonal chambers. Paper wasp nests are commonly found hanging in undisturbed corners of our homes, on walls, windowsills or even among plants.

Potter wasp

☐ A nest that looks like a tiny clay pot. You may find this on a plant pot, window grill or outdoor furniture. Potter wasps collect balls of wet mud and sculpt the pot using their mouthparts.

* Wasps are fascinating creatures but they don't like to be disturbed. Keep a safe distance from them and their nests!

Black Mud-dauber Wasp

☐ Tube-like mud nests on walls and windowsills. Sometimes, these nests will have stripes made from different-coloured mud.

Hornet's nest

☐ Large nests made from plant fibres, looking like papier-mâché lanterns, present in rock crevices or hanging from trees and ceilings. These nests have a thick covering over the cells to protect the larvae, and the opening at the bottom is guarded carefully. They are built by hornets, a group of large-sized paper wasps.

Spider wasp

☐ Tiny openings in the ground, dug or discovered by spider wasps. These wasps catch spiders and drag them into their burrows, lay a single egg on the spider's body and seal the nest.

Blue Mud-dauber Wasp

☐ Small, circular holes sealed with mud in wooden furniture, walls and even electrical sockets! Mud-dauber wasps lay their eggs in cavities, fill them with food for their unborn larvae and seal them up. They also use abandoned nests of other wasps.

Has a grassy neighbourhood park ever left you wondering:

Do grasses only grow in parks and lawns?

In parks and playgrounds, roadsides and gardens – grass is all around us. But did you know that grasses also grow in many other places? They can be found in forests, agricultural fields, and even form their own unique habitats!

A diverse family

Apart from the kind that is grown in parks and lawns, there are many different types of grasses. The largest grasses are bamboos, which can grow as tall as a 10-storey building! Entire forests of tall, creaking bamboo exist in Southern and North-Eastern India. In contrast, there are also large areas around the world that are covered in grasses the height of your knee, with hardly any trees or shrubs. These ecosystems are natural grasslands and make up about one-fourth of India's total land area. They are home to thousands of creatures – insects, rodents, birds and even large animals like wolves, blackbuck and rhinos, all of whom depend on them for food, shelter and a home!

Stems

All grasses have hollow stems that are blocked off at nodes. New stems grow from each node – which means that even if grass is cut or eaten from the top, it can grow back again from the next node. Grasses have evolved this way so that they can keep growing even after being grazed on by animals. Humans use the hollow, flexible stems of bamboo to construct furniture and even buildings, while beetles, bats, rodents and sometimes even tarantula spiders use these hollows as homes.

Flowers, fruits and seeds

Grass flowers don't rely on animals for pollination and so, don't have to be showy or fragrant. Instead, their tiny pollen is carried from one flower to another by gusts of wind. After pollination, the flowers transform into fruit and seeds. If you enjoy eating roasted corn, you've eaten the seeds of a common grass fruit! Grains like rice, wheat and millets are all part of the grass family, and are found in kitchens around the world. Birds like sparrows and munias have developed short stout beaks that are specially adapted to eating grains. You may have seen these birds fluttering around in search of their favourite food in open markets or near agricultural fields.

Leaves

Next time you come across any grass, try tearing the leaves horizontally and vertically. Which one is easier to do? Grasses have long, slender leaves which are called blades. The little veins inside the leaf are all parallel to each other, making it easy to tear the leaf into vertical strips. This detail comes in handy for weaverbirds – like the Baya – who tear long strips of grass to create their intricately woven nests.

Some grasses like lemongrass and vetiver have a distinct scent which discourages insects from eating their leaves. Humans love these smells and use them to make perfumes, lotions and even insect repellants.

Grains from the grass family, like wheat, rice, millets and corn, are all called **cereals**.

Baya Weaver

Grasses might be a part of your life as well! Search for different grasses around you. Ask adults to guide you and help you read the labels on products. Try and find at least one from each row and tick the ones you have found.

Flowers, seeds and fruits	Stem	Leaves	Invisible grass
 Grass broom	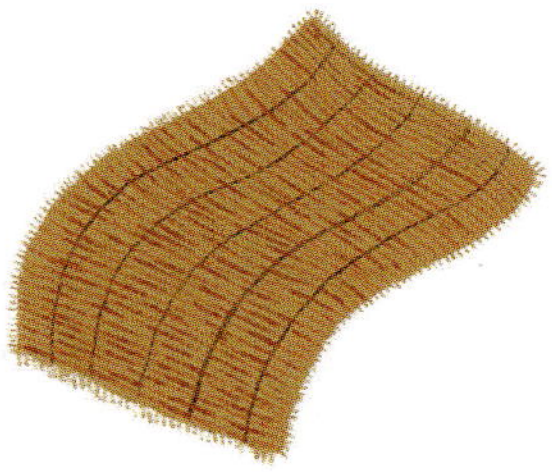 Mats or blinds	 Lemongrass as a herb or in a tea	 Soap, cream or other products with lemongrass, khus or vetiver
 Grains like rice, wheat and millets	 Bamboo furniture	 Ornamental grass or bamboo	 Sugar or jaggery made from sugarcane
 Corn, babycorn or popcorn	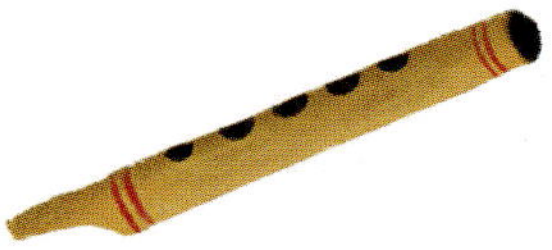 Flute	 Woven ornaments and baskets	 Insect repellents with citronella

Have you ever seen a bird carrying a stick and wondered:

Do all birds use twigs to build nests?

Most species of birds build nests and they all do it for the same reasons – to have a safe space to lay eggs and raise their young till they are able to fly away on their own. But are all bird nests cup-shaped and made of twigs like the ones we see in storybooks?

Red-whiskered Bulbul

> While a baby chick grows inside the egg, the parent birds keep the egg warm until it hatches. This is called **incubation**. Most birds do this by sitting on their eggs.

Leaves and grasses

Some birds are expert weavers, and use leaves and grasses to make their nests.

The male Baya Weaver constructs a hanging nest using hundreds of blades of grass. These nests are often built at the tips of thin branches or palm fronds which won't support the weight of predators trying to reach them.

Tailorbirds stitch broad leaves into a cup shape using plant fibres or spider silk. The nest looks so much like just another leaf of a plant that predators often fail to spot it.

The inside and outside

Birds often line the inside of their nests with soft material like feathers, animal hair, mosses, lichens, spider webs, soft grass or human-made items like thread, cotton, cloth and sometimes even plastic. This keeps the nest warm and comfortable for the newly hatched chicks.

The outside of the nest is most visible to potential predators, and birds often camouflage their nests using materials similar to their surroundings. For example, ground nesting birds often use stones or grasses to make their nests hard to spot.

Sticks, branches, trunks (and twigs!)

Many birds use woody materials from trees to make their nests.

Bulbuls and crows build twig nests that cup their eggs and keep them from falling.

Birds like parakeets, barbets and owlets nest in holes in tree trunks, which are often hard to spot and are also sheltered from wind and rain.

Clay and mud

Birds are sculptors, too, and some of them use clay or mud to build their nests. Once the mud dries, it is firm and holds its shape.

Swifts and swallows use little balls of wet mud to build nests on cliffs, bridges and even buildings. The mud nest can be built on vertical or upside-down surfaces which are difficult for predators to access.

Bee-eaters dig tunnels in sandbanks and lay their eggs at the end of the tunnel. They sometimes nest in large groups.

Birds live in many different habitats and use whatever material they find to create the best possible nest. They build, weave, sculpt and stitch sturdy and intricate nests using only their feet and beaks!

Can you identify the material used for building these nests?

Blue-tailed Bee-eater

✏ ....

Olive-backed Sunbird

✏ ....

Rose-ringed Parakeet

✏ ....

Tailorbird

✏ ....

You will need

- Nest building materials that are available to you – except twigs

- Materials from your home such as bits of string, cotton or cloth – make sure they are things that a bird could use!

- 2 walnuts/small onions/potatoes or anything else that is roughly the same weight as a small egg

- A pair of scissors (since humans don't have beaks or claws)

1. Throughout this activity, imagine that you are a bird who needs to build a nest. To build like a bird, you can only use your thumb and first finger (except while using the scissors).

2. Using the materials you have collected, build a nest for yourself. The nest must be strong enough to protect eggs from wind, rains, the cold, and also predators.

3. While building, test your nest by sprinkling water on it. Does it get damaged by water? Will it get cold and wet? If so, pick different materials and keep trying!

4. Keep testing how strong your nest is by placing your 2 egg-like objects in it. Does it hold the weight?

5. When you are happy with your nest, choose an outdoor space to keep it where it will be hard to see for predators.

✏ What materials did you use to build the nest?

....
....

✏ Where did you place your nest? Why did you choose to place it there?

....
....
....
....

Have you ever seen a bird arranging its feathers and wondered:

Why does a bird have different types of feathers?

Do these feathers look familiar?

They all belong to the ordinary pigeon, and you may have seen them outside your home, on a windowsill or maybe even in a stray cat's mouth. You can often tell one type of bird from another from their differently shaped or coloured feathers. But why does an individual bird have different types of feathers on its body?

 Just like humans, birds have bacteria and mites that live on their skin. Always wash your hands after handling feathers!

You will need

- An envelope or paper bag
- A bowl of water
- A sheet of paper

1. Walk around your neighbourhood or a nearby park and collect 5 feathers in the envelope. Search under trees, and beside walls and ledges where birds perch. Try to find ones that look and feel different from each other.

2. Try out the following tests with each of the feathers and note your observations.

✎ Blow on the feather. Does it change shape or bend?
1 ....
2 ....
3 ....
4 ....
5 ....

✎ Feel the feather with your fingers. Does it feel smooth, fluffy, or both?
1 ....
2 ....
3 ....
4 ....
5 ....

✎ Hold the feather out under bright sunlight and rotate it. Does the colour change?
1 ....
2 ....
3 ....
4 ....
5 ....

✎ Dip the feather in water for 5 seconds. Does the feather get fully wet?
1 ....
2 ....
3 ....
4 ....
5 ....

✎ What are features shared by most or even all of the feathers you found?
....
....
....
....
....
....

Feathers are a bird's best friend

Birds are the only animals that have feathers – which help them in many ways!

You may have noticed that the feathers you collected have a central stick-like shaft, attached to which are tiny branches called barbs.

On the bigger feathers, the barbs are firm and stitched together like tiny zippers, forming a smooth surface. The firm shaft of the feather doesn't bend even in strong wind. These feathers are found on the wings and tail of the bird, and help the bird fly – which is why they are called **flight feathers**.

Flight feathers

Shaft
Barbs

Down feathers

Under the brightly coloured feathers, birds have a layer of much smaller feathers with soft barbs. These are called **down feathers** and act like an undershirt, keeping the bird warm.

A scientist who studies birds is called an **ornithologist**, and would not mind being called a 'birdbrain'!

Contour feathers

Some feathers have a mixture of both firm and soft barbs, and are smaller than the tail and wing feathers. These are called **contour feathers**, and are found on parts of the bird's body other than the tail and wings. They give the bird its colour and pattern.

Some feathers shine with fantastic colours as the angle of light reflecting off their barbs changes. This phenomenon is called **iridescence**. Peacocks, sunbirds and even the familiar pigeons have some iridescent feathers.

Some birds use the colours and patterns on their feathers to hide from predators, while others use them to attract mates or to scare off their rivals. As you may have observed, feathers with firm barbs also repel water, acting like a colourful raincoat.

Have you ever seen a dragonfly lift off in the blink of an eye and wondered:

What makes dragonflies such amazing pilots?

Every year, the rains are accompanied by swarms of web-winged dragonflies. They are amazing hunters who catch prey in mid-air. They can also fly backwards and upside down, and are fast enough to keep pace with a car. What's the secret to their amazing skills on the wing?

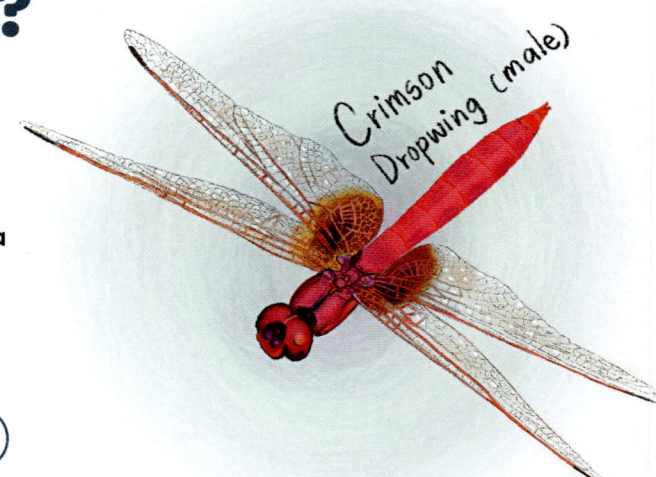

You will need

- An A4 size sheet
- A paper clip

1 Using the following instructions, make a paper plane.

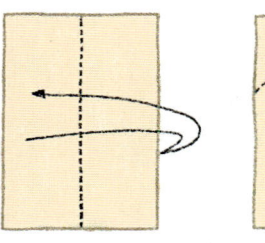 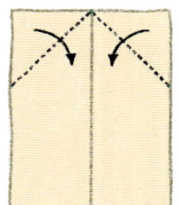 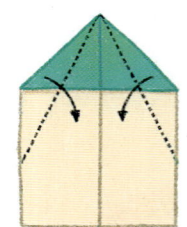

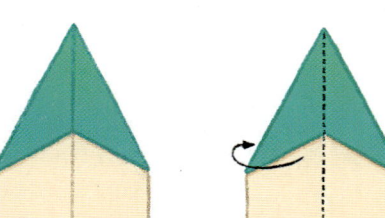 

2 Find a space free of obstructions and wind that might block or disturb the plane's flight.

3 Launch the plane a few times. Try and get it as far as possible!

4 Now, attach a paper clip to your plane. Launch the plane a few more times. Pay attention to how it feels to launch and how it flies.

 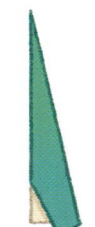 

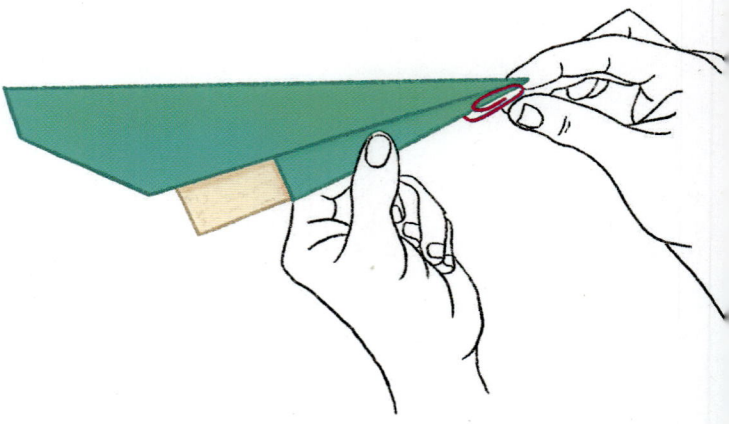

✎ Did the plane feel different after attaching the paper clip? In what way?

....
....
....
....
....

✎ Did it fly differently after attaching the paper clip? How?

....
....
....
....
....

A creature worth copying

Observing nature has taught scientists a lot about building better machines. The dragonfly is one such example – by observing the dragonfly, engineers have been able to create hovering drones with flapping wings.

You may have noticed that after attaching the paper clip to your aeroplane, it was easier to launch and flew a little straighter than before. This is because the paper clip added a little bit of weight in just the right place. Similarly, if you observe the front edge of a dragonfly's wing, there is a small coloured spot which is thicker than the rest of the wing. This adds a tiny amount of weight to the front of their wings, helping the dragonfly balance in the air and glide. The curved surface and edges of the wing also help them turn quickly while flying, making them glorious acrobats of the air.

Eyes nearly touch each other

Thick body

Wings open and away from the body when resting

Strong and fast fliers

Globe Skimmer dragonfly (male)

Wings closed and above their bodies when resting

Slower fliers than dragonflies

Eyes on either side of the head

Thin body

Marsh Bluetail damselfly (male)

Meet the cousins

Damselflies are close cousins of dragonflies, and are also talented pilots. Like dragonflies they have slightly thicker spots on all four of their wings. Both dragonflies and damselflies are commonly found near freshwater bodies like ponds and lakes, as they lay their eggs in the water. The larvae live underwater and come out from the water as winged adults.

Around the World

Dragonflies have been zooming around the earth since there were dinosaurs—except back then their wings were about the same size as those of a crow! Today's dragonflies are just as amazing, but in different ways. One species called the Globe Skimmer undertakes a remarkable feat of migration over the Indian Ocean. These finger-sized insects fly all the way from India to eastern Africa. After reaching Africa, they breed there and their babies grow up to have babies of their own. A few months later, the great-great-grandchildren of the ones that left India return to lay eggs here.

> Scientists and engineers use observations and learnings from nature to create machines, materials and technology. This field is called **biomimicry**.

Have you ever heard the telltale fluttering outside your window and wondered:

Why are there so many pigeons everywhere?!

Railings, windowsills, staircases, terraces, ledges, balconies and washing lines – sounds like pigeon paradise! You probably see (or hear) at least one pigeon every day – picking at scraps, collecting sticks for a nest, or resting between meals. Their constant presence around us has made them a big part of our lives, whether we like it or not! But why are pigeons so drawn to our cities?

You will need: A pen or pencil

1. Choose a building where you have seen pigeons before. It could be your own home, apartment or school, or a friend's house.

2. Divide the building into different sections – the ground, roof, windows, balcony, ledges, staircases and so on, depending on how the space looks.

3. Search each section of the building for signs of pigeons – feathers, poop, piles of sticks, the gurgling call, and the birds themselves!

4. Note the types of signs in each space.

✏️ Where did you notice the *most* signs of pigeons?

....
....
....

✏️ Where did you notice the *fewest* signs of pigeons?

....
....
....

Our feathery neighbours

You may have seen lots of pigeons around buildings, but they weren't always here. Thousands of years ago, humans found pigeons living on rock cliffs, building their nests on ledges and in stony outcrops. They thought these birds were very beautiful and brought them home as pets. Soon, pigeons became favourite pets around the world and were even kept in the homes of royalty! Over time, some of these birds escaped and bred with wild pigeons around them. They had become used to food provided by humans and flocked to wherever they could easily find it, such as cities, towns and villages. To them, buildings are like rock cliffs with plenty of places to nest, and there is delicious food everywhere – in waste bins, and in gardens and parks, where people come especially to feed them.

Like pigeons, many animals can find their way back home or breeding spots from unfamiliar, faraway places. This ability is called **homing**.

Finding their way

Even when released many kilometres away from their home, pigeons can find their way back! In the past, they were trained to carry messages including vital information during times of war and conflict. Through years of research, scientists have learnt that pigeons use a variety of techniques to find their way. They use the position of the sun as a compass, and can identify the direction in which sunlight travels even on cloudy days. They also recognise and remember landmarks around them. Using the earth's magnetic field, and perhaps even sound and smell, pigeons create a mental map to navigate their surroundings. So next time you need directions, try asking a local pigeon?

Have you ever come across a pungent pile of animal poo and wondered:

Who pooped?

Every animal that eats, poops! You may not be able to see or hear an animal, but you know it's been there because of what it left behind.

THIS IS MY TERRITORY
I am here!
I am healthy!

Poop scientists

Poop is very useful to scientists who study animals. In India, one way in which forest officers count the number of tigers in an area is by keeping track of their poop. Through DNA tests, they can find out exactly which tiger did the deed, and by extension, the number of tigers in the area. After studying the poop further, scientists can answer questions such as 'What did it eat?', 'Is the tiger healthy?' and even 'Is it going to have cubs?'!

Waste or not?

What goes in, must come out – end of story! Or is it? Apart from cleaning their stomachs, poop can be very useful to animals. Some birds like storks and vultures poop on their own feet to keep cool. In fact, their poop acts as an antibacterial wash which protects them from diseases. Animals like tigers, lions, and even dogs and cats use poop to mark their territory. In nature, stinky poop is a message from the pooper – 'This is my place, don't come around here!' Some animals bury their poop so that bigger animals don't find them intruding on their territory. On the other hand, animals like goats and deer poop small pellets which have little or no smell, making them harder for hungry predators to sniff out. Birds and bats eat fruit and poop out undigested seeds, which grow into new plants. And finally, poop can be a resource for other animals, like dung beetles which collect poop, roll it into a ball and lay their own eggs in it.

Dung beetle

> Animal poop has many names! Carnivore poop is called **scat**. Big herbivores (like elephants and cows) make **dung**, while smaller herbivores (like deer and hares) and birds leave **droppings**. Seabird and bat poop is called **guano**.

1. Choose a defined area – it could be your home, your street, a park, etc.
2. Look around for different kinds of poop. Some of the common ones are listed here. Tick them as you find them!
3. Document your findings like an ecologist on a scat survey:

✏️ Area surveyed

....

✏️ Duration

....

✏️ Number of poop signs found and which animal they belong to

....
....
....
....

If you're not too grossed out, pour water on the poop or poke it with a stick. Is it fresh or dry? This should give you an idea of whether the animal was there a short or long time ago. You may also see seeds or insect legs, indicating what the animal has eaten.

○ **Gecko poop** can be found on the walls or behind furniture. The black part is food waste and the white bit is actually pee!

○ **Rat, mouse and bandicoot poop** can be found near dustbins or food storage areas.

✱ All poop, including human poop, contains bacteria and other microbes. Don't handle poop with your hands and always wash up if you touch it by accident.

○ Birds poop and pee at the same time – so a **bird poop** will always contain some liquid when fresh. You may find it on railings, and under windows, tree branches and other places they roost.

○ **Cat and dog poop** look similar, although cat poop is smaller and harder to find since they often bury or cover it.

○ **Earthworm poop** can be found in muddy areas, especially during rainy weather, and is a sign of healthy soil.

○ **Bat poop** can be found under trees or ceilings in dark areas with footholds for the bats to hang from. The only times that bats are not hanging upside down is when they pull themselves upright to give birth or poop!

○ **Cow poop** typically contains a lot of fibre from the greens cows eat. This makes it an excellent fertiliser and in some parts of India, it is even used as cement!

Have you noticed the same kind of plant growing in different spots and wondered:

How do seeds reach new places?

With the right mix of water, sunlight, soil and air, every little seed can grow into a gorgeous plant. But how do plants make sure that their seeds find everything they need to grow?

You will need

- 2 green moong dal seeds (or any whole seed you can easily find)
- Firm card paper
- A pair of scissors
- Glue
- Chalk
- Measuring tape

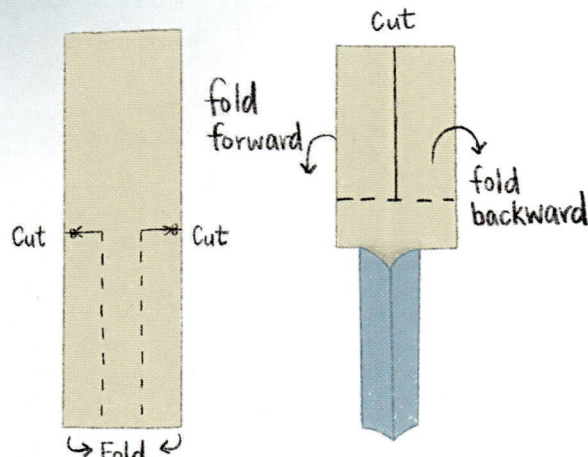

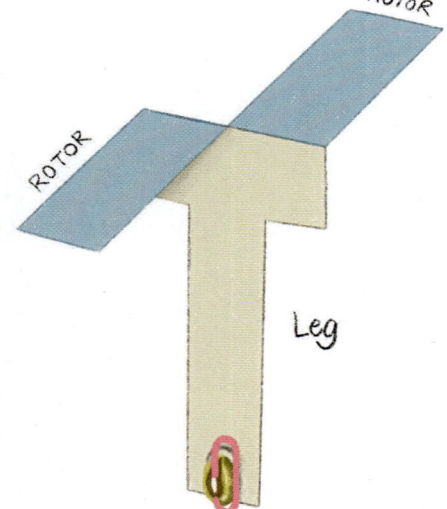

1. For this activity, let's pretend you are a tree. Look for a safe spot at least 10 feet above the ground, like the top of a slide, a balcony or a terrace. This space is your 'treetop'. Make sure the ground below is flat and undisturbed, with a straight drop.

2. Now, mark the ground directly under you with chalk. This is the 'base' of your tree.

3. Using the paper and scissors, make a helicopter as shown on the right. Stick one seed at the bottom of the helicopter with glue. This is your 'Flying Seed'.

4. The other seed is your 'Falling Seed'.

5. From your treetop, launch the Flying Seed so that it reaches the ground.

6. Drop the Falling Seed straight down so that it hits the ground.

7. Mark where your Falling Seed landed with chalk. Measure the distance between the seed and the base of the 'tree'.

8. Measure the distance between the base and where Flying Seed landed in its helicopter.

9. You can repeat this activity a few more times to see if you have similar or different results.

✎ Which seed (Falling or Flying) was further away from the base mark?

....

✎ How can you make these seeds go even further away from your 'tree'?

....
....
....
....

Plants try to spread their seeds over a wide area so that each seed has its own space to grow. This is called **seed dispersal**.

Falling seeds

Some plants drop their seeds straight down, just like your Falling Seeds did! If a seed lands on moist soil, it grows. But if it falls too close to its parent plant or to other seeds, they all have to share the same patch of sunlight and soil – meaning less nutrition for everyone.

🔍 *Why do plants need sunlight? More on page 18.*

Helicopter Tree

Flying seeds

Did your Flying Seeds land further away from your 'tree' than the Falling Seeds? Could the helicopter have helped? Plants use a similar trick very effectively. Some trees have seeds with wings so that they can float along with the wind. The Helicopter Tree is found across most of South India and is named after the shape of its seeds.

Giant Milkweed seeds have a wispy tail which makes them float in the air. When their ripe and dry pods crack open, they release hundreds of flying seeds.

Giant Milkweed

Mexican Petunia

Exploding pods

You may have thought of throwing the seeds so that they land further away and have more space to grow. Plants know how to throw seeds, too, and some have seed pods that pop with force. The Mexican Petunia is a flower you can find in parks and gardens. When the dry seed pods get wet with dew or rain, they burst open with a loud pop, scattering the seeds widely.

Floating seeds

Some plants rely on water to take their seeds to new places, like seagoing explorers. The Coconut seed has a hard, husky shell that can float on water. Coastal Coconut seeds that fall into the ocean can float for a long time to reach distant shores where they take root.

Coconut

Travelling in exchange for food

Does your favourite fruit have a seed inside it? That's the plant's way of making sure the seed is dispersed. A hungry human, bird, bat or other fruit eater will eat the delicious fruit pulp and throw the seed away, hopefully far from the parent plant. Small seeds are sometimes swallowed whole and travel long distances in an animal's stomach. When the animal poops, the seed comes out surrounded by nutritious manure, ready to start its life.

Hitchhiking!

Plants can't walk around like animals, so they take lifts! Some seeds have small barbs that hook onto a passing animal's fur, like velcro does. They travel with the animal and land wherever it chooses to them off. These seeds also hitchhike on human shoes and clothes. If you see Bristlegrass nearby, do it a favour by sneakily sticking the seed's head to a friend's bag or T-shirt!

Bristlegrass

Have you ever heard tales about blood-sucking bats and wondered:

What do bats really eat?

Books, movies and ghost stories often feature bats that drink blood – but how true are these tales? When a bat wakes up from a good day's sleep at sunset, what will it eat for breakfast?

While searching for food, bats may accidentally enter our homes. If this happens, avoid direct physical contact, turn off the light and fans, and open a window to let the bat out.

Some bats map their surroundings by emitting frequent, high-pitched calls. The calls bounce off objects and back to the bat's ears, helping it understand how far, big or fast an object is. This way of making a map with sounds is called **echolocation**.

You will need

-  A torch
- A paper and pencil

1. Find working street lights and fruiting trees in your neighbourhood.

2. At dusk, ask an adult to accompany you and spend time observing the streetlights and fruiting trees for bats. If you don't see bats zipping by a tree or lamp, move to the next one.

3. If you see bats visiting lamps or trees, spend at least 15 minutes observing the space. Note down what the bats are doing, and how big they are. You can compare the size to birds you recognise.

4. Observe the canopy of the trees visited by bats. Are there fruits or flowers on the tree? Take a look on the ground under the tree and note down what you see there as well.

5. Observe the streetlamp – do you see any movement around the light?

✎ What did you observe on and under the tree?
....
....
....

✎ Why do you think bats visit fruiting trees?
....
....
....

✎ What did you observe around the light?
....
....
....

✎ Why do you think bats fly around street lamps?
....
....
....

Indian Flying Fox eating mango

Midnight snackers

Most bats are nocturnal – they sleep during the day and are active at night. They rest by hanging upside down, some in trees and others in sheltered places like caves or buildings. They might roost alone or in small groups, but some cave-dwelling bats gather in thousands (and even millions) to take shelter as they sleep.

You may have seen large, fox-faced bats hanging from the branches of fruiting trees. Like these Flying Foxes, many bats love eating fruits, including some of our favourites like litchees, jamuns, guavas, papayas, dates and bananas. This group of bats is known as fruit bats. They hang from branches and chomp away at the fruit, dropping seeds that are too big to eat. When they eat fruit with small seeds, the seeds pass through their stomachs undigested and are pooped out. If the seeds land in a suitable place, they can grow into new trees, and soon, more fruit! Some tropical seeds are actually more likely to grow when they pass through a bat's digestive system. You can thank bats for your summer jamuns!

Other sweet-toothed bats skip the fruits and focus on flowers – they slurp up delicious nectar from the base of the flower. They are known as nectarivorous bats or nectar-feeding bats. While the bat moves from flower to flower, pollen grains stick to its body and are transferred from one flower to another. Bat-pollinated trees like mango and guava trees have strong-smelling flowers that are pale or white so that they are easily visible in the dark. Fruit bats and nectar-feeding bats find food using their exceptional eyesight and sense of smell. On average, they are large in size and some can be as big as a crow – earning them the nickname **'megabats'**.

Cave Nectar Bat feeding on banana flower

Fulvus Leaf-nosed Bat

echolocation

Termite

🔍 What's 'pollination'? More on **page 40**.

Some bats are carnivorous – they eat insects, and small animals like scorpions, frogs, fish and even other bats. There are also three species of bats in South America that feed on the blood of other animals, but they don't come in contact with humans. Most carnivorous bats prefer meals of the six-legged kind and catch insects like moths, beetles and mosquitos mid-flight! They flock to places that attract insects, like crop fields, water bodies and – as you may have observed – street lamps. Insect-eating bats are also called **'microbats'** because most are the size of a sparrow or smaller. They also have large ears to find their prey using echolocation. Next time you eat chocolate, remember that a bat probably helped the cacao plant grow healthy and strong by feeding on cacao-eating bugs!

Have you ever taken a walk in your neighbourhood and wondered:

Which trees are growing around me?

Trees are all around us! They grow from seeds that may have travelled far from their parent tree – carried by wind, water or animals. But sometimes, travelling humans also bring seeds with them from other countries – sometimes deliberately, but at other times, at the bottom of their shoes or stuck to their clothes. If the seeds find a comfortable place to grow, they take root in their new home. We see our surroundings change with the seasons as flowers bloom, leaves shed and new leaves grow on trees' branches. Their fruits make their way into our favourite dishes, their leaves and flowers brighten our festival celebrations. Sometimes, they lead to fun games, too!

Try and find one or more of these lovely trees around you.

Settle a bet!

The Silk Cotton is a tall tree with large red flowers that have five fleshy petals. The tree grows from tiny black seeds which come with a parachute of fluffy cotton, allowing them to be carried by the wind. Like other flowers, the Silk Cotton flower has long stalks in the centre of the flower, called stamens. At the top of the stamen, there is a small black head that carries pollen. The anthers of silk cotton can be used to settle a bet!

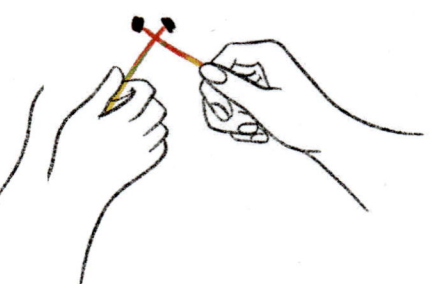
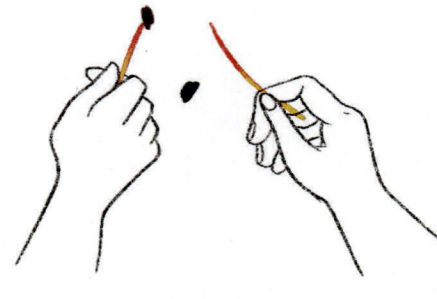

1 Hold the stamen at the base and give a second stamen to your friend.

2 Interlock the heads, and pull! Whoever pulls the other person's head off, wins!

Monster claws

Gulmohar is a tree found all over India, although it is originally from the forests of Madagascar. It has wide branches and bright red flowers which take over the whole tree when it is in bloom. It also has long, woody seed pods. Gulmohar flowers often bloom in the rainy season, and the fallen buds and petals make a natural red carpet under the tree. The bud is protected by green leaf-like structures called sepals. Make yourself a set of monster claws using these!

Leafy handbags

Ashoka trees are commonly found planted along roads. The Ashoka tree has long, slender leaves. The fruits are a favourite of bats and birds, and the leaves are used to decorate homes during festivals. The leaves can also be crafted into a fun little handbag!

1 Curve the stem

2 Wrap B around A

3 Pull the tip of A over B and through the loop

4 Tuck the tip of A into B

Musical leaves

We see Coconut trees both in and around our homes, especially in South India. They are such a part of a town's fabric that people often build their houses around existing Coconut trees, with a hole in the ceiling to make room for the tree to grow through. Coconut fruits and leaves are often used in ceremonies and for decoration. Like grasses, Coconut leaves have parallel veins, so they can easily be torn into strips and used to weave decorations. They can also be used to make whistles!

1 Wrap A around B, starting tight, and loosening to a cone shape

2 Push C through A to hold it in place

3 BLOW!

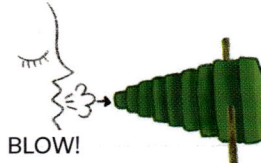

What trees did you find around your home? Ask relatives, friends and neighbours for more fun crafts and activities they know of with your hometown's trees and plants.

Create a Nature Map

Document nature around you and be a Neighbourhood Naturalist!

You will need (A pen or pencil)

1 Prepare your pages
In each circle drawn in the following pages, write the names of places you hope to explore through the activities in this book. These could include 'My Home', 'My Street', 'My Park', 'My School', etc. Leave a few circles blank, or draw new circles in case the book takes you to unexpected places!

2 Document your sightings
As you complete the activities in the book, you will observe and learn to identify plants, animals and other living things around you. When you spot something you recognise, find the corresponding sticker in the sticker sheets at the end of the book and stick it next to the label of the place where you saw it.

You can also document your observations of living creatures on online platforms like iNaturalist (inaturalist.org) and India Biodiversity Portal (indiabiodiversity.org). Here, you can upload photos you have clicked and get the species identified with a little help from AI and human experts. If you would like to help scientists understand how the seasonality of flowering and fruiting of trees is changing, consider signing up at SeasonWatch (seasonwatch.in). And if you are a budding birdwatcher, you can use tools like Merlin (merlin.allaboutbirds.org) and eBird (ebird.org) to explore and document the birds around you. All this helps scientists and other nature enthusiasts to better understand the world and how it is changing!

Nature Map

Nature Map

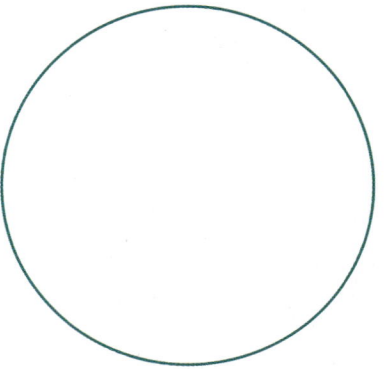

Nature Map

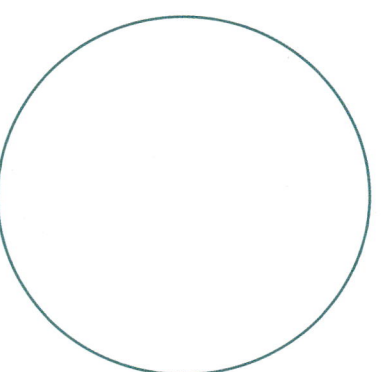

Nature Map

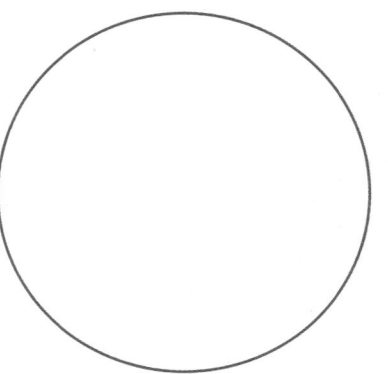

Nature Map

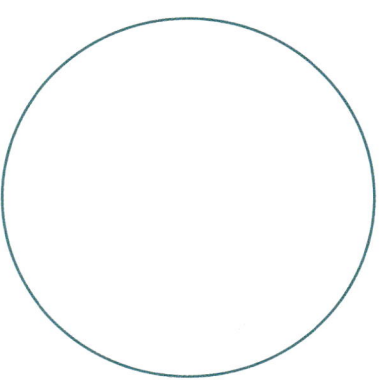

Nature Map

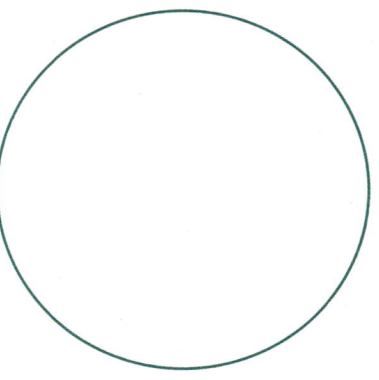

Nature Map

Nature Map

The team

AUTHOR AND EDITOR
Vena Kapoor
vena.kapoor@gmail.com

I am constantly mesmerised, chuffed and in awe of the natural world, and channel this through Nature Classrooms. I have an unexplainable special place in my head and heart for spiders and insects hiding in plain sight.

AUTHOR AND EDITOR
Suhel Quader
suhelq@ncf-india.org

When I'm not outdoors looking at birds and trees, I try to get more people – children and adults – to notice and love the natural world around us.

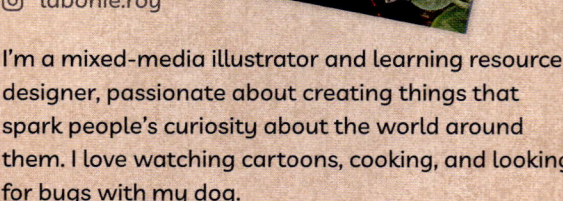

AUTHOR AND ART DIRECTOR
Labonie Roy
🅞 labonie.roy

I'm a mixed-media illustrator and learning resource designer, passionate about creating things that spark people's curiosity about the world around them. I love watching cartoons, cooking, and looking for bugs with my dog.

DESIGNER
Pratyush Gupta
🅞 swarpeti

I'm an interdisciplinary designer, Hindustani vocalist and the author of *Swarpeti*, a pop-up book series on Indian classical music. Weaving information with music and storytelling, I craft magical experiences that celebrate nature and culture.

ILLUSTRATOR
Tanrus
🅞 tanrus.studio

I am a multidisciplinary artist whose work is spread across art, design and film. My current focus is on illustration, lettering, paper craft, embroidery and clay art to create children's content, which reflects my love for nature and underwater life.

ILLUSTRATOR
Upasana Chadha
🅞 tequila.and.paints

I am a multimedia illustrator and storyteller. My practice is primarily based on children's books and publications, but I enjoy taking on diverse projects. I have worked in many industries such as publishing, non-profit, educational, social media and editorial.

About NCF

The Nature Conservation Foundation is a research, education and conservation action organisation, established as a public charitable trust in 1996. Our work focuses on bringing innovative research and imaginative solutions to the conservation of India's wildlife heritage. As part of this, we also work with the public on nature and wildlife, engaging children and adults in ecological observation as well as developing and distributing nature learning material.

About Indian Pitta Kids

Indian Pitta Kids is part of the Indian Pitta imprint. Our books about birds, wildlife and natural history for young readers showcase animals, habitats and landscapes from India. The books combine authentic natural history, information, interesting facts, stunning photos and illustrations to spark interest and feed curiosity about the magnificent birds and animals that call India home.

'*Be a Neighbourhood Naturalist* provides a terrific way to re-engage with biodiversity in your locality, from plants and spiders to mushrooms and frogs – and even the annoying fly!'

– **Harini Nagendra,** author, ecologist and educator

'Nature is the biggest lab and there are so many secrets to be explored at home and in your immediate neighbourhood. I would wholeheartedly recommend this easy-to-read book, with exquisite illustrations and simple activities, to each and every budding naturalist.'

– **Arvind Gupta,** science educator, toy inventor and author